A Gleam of Light

A Gleam of Light

The Trials and Triumphs of a Century of Missionary Work in Morocco

Ila Marie Davis

with Evelyn Stenbock–Ditty

Gospel Missionary Union
Kansas City, Missouri

Requests for information should be addressed to:
Gospel Missionary Union
10000 North Oak Trafficway
Kansas City, MO 64155

Editors: Noelle Melito and Michele Phillips
Design and production: Ron Zuercher

ISBN: 1-890940-02-X

Printed in the United States of America

"Lift up your eyes, Morocco,
for a gleam of light is coming to you!"

Henry Hammer
GMU missionary
1894

Contents

Foreword

Ila Davis, a GMU missionary of the highest caliber, was a lady who removed the uncertainties of the Great Commission response to Islam. "Liela," as she was affectionately known, writes of her nearly half a century of mission service in Meknes, Morocco, a fanatical Muslim city in the heart of the "10/40 Window" of unreached peoples. One cannot read her story without saying, "Yes!" and "Amen! It can be done!" Rather than an account of "how it used to be," we have an account of "how it can be." Faith at work, coupled with perseverance, brings glory to God. It is the way the Muslim world will finally bow to Jesus Christ.

It was my privilege, along with my family, to work with Ila in Meknes for several years. During that period, from 1967 to 1973, many laborers came enthusiastically and left despairingly. But Ila persevered! That tenacity ultimately wins the day for God's glory.

Derb Skat, Ila's home, was a dead–end street. In reality, however, it was an opening for many to a new street: a pathway to God. Ila was there – always there – pointing the way to the One who is the Way, the Truth and the Life and who said, "No one comes to the Father except through me" (John 14:6).

Today's missionary enthusiasts face more uncertainty than history has ever recorded. The world is no friend of the gospel. Islam is shaking its fist in the shadow of the cross, making a final effort to hold back the advance of God's Kingdom. North Africa, an ancient site of vibrant Christian faith, continues its attempt to wear down and intimidate apostles of Christ and His gospel. Ila Davis persevered, leaving us a legacy worth following.

Ila's last work was also one of persistence. She continued her manuscript for this book, even when struck with heart problems. Once the manuscript was completed and sent to the mission headquarters for final editing, Ila stepped beyond the "dead-end street" right into the presence of God. She moved on to her eternal reward within days of completing her manuscript.

This is the kind of faith that removes mountains. Read and be blessed by the life of a 20th-century saint. "And the Lord will deliver me from every evil work and preserve me for His heavenly kingdom. To Him be glory forever and ever. Amen!" (2 Timothy 4:18 NKJV).

J. Ray Tallman, D. Miss.
International Director, Arab World Ministries

Acknowledgements

My special thanks to Derek and Shaman Parks, who encouraged me and gave me a start in writing; to Ruth and Fred Fox, who read and reread the manuscripts; to Mary Bell, who also read and edited some chapters.

I am grateful for Rev. and Mrs. Howard Brumme, who encouraged me at every turn and gave suggestions. They helped me buy a word processor and gave time to teach me to use it.

I owe special thanks to Gospel Missionary Union, especially to Abe Reddekopp, Vice President of North America Ministries, for handling the many details.

Special thanks also goes to Evelyn Stenbock–Ditty, who took over the writing and added so much information. I am grateful for the editorial help of several colleagues who worked with me in Morocco, ensuring accuracy of details and offering their various points of view: Rev. John M. Barcus, Rev. Robert C. Schneider, Rev. Peter Z. and Wilma Harder Friesen and Rev. Gordon McRostie.

Finally, my grateful thanks to the many friends who encouraged me by waiting patiently for the finished project.

Chapter 1

Morocco: My Country!

The poet Edna St. Vincent Millay wrote, "Thou'st made the world too beautiful . . . My soul is all but out of me!" Such a day, common in Morocco, arose one morning in the winter of 1956. I was working with British missionaries, educating young Moroccan women who had converted to Christianity. A young colleague and I were in Tangier, Morocco, on a business trip to the British hospital compound. The hospital sat on a bluff overlooking the Straits of Gibraltar, the western entrance to the Mediterranean Sea. From our room in the guest house, we could dimly see the great Rock of Gibraltar and the coast of Spain across the shimmering blue water.

During the bus trip north from central Morocco, we bought huge, sweet navel oranges at a rest stop for a penny a pound. The aroma of barbecued shish–kebabs, the crush and confusion of the crowded bus, the turbaned men and veiled women – this kaleidoscope of new sights and sounds amazed my companion. Leathery–faced people yelled to and at each other, then moments later redeemed themselves with broad smiles, setting their brown eyes to twinkling.

If I close my eyes, I can still see the women, bent double beneath their immense loads, bundles of sticks lashed to their backs. What was a woman worth in Morocco? A bearer of children and a bearer of burdens – crushing burdens that break the hearts of mothers everywhere, to be sure, but physical burdens as well. A strong young man would have to hoist the heavy bundles onto a woman's back.

Around the bus station, half–clad, runny–nosed children were tied on their mothers' backs, toddling along behind them or roughhousing unsupervised with other vagabonds in the streets. Children everywhere! Even on the bus they raised their cranky voices, and nothing but their mother's breast could quiet them.

The bus trip was excellent orientation for my young companion, providing a great deal of exposure to and experience in the Moroccan culture. In contrast, the clear, beautiful morning beckoned us to follow the rugged path from the compound to the seashore, to a quiet world of ocean breezes and gentle waves. Relaxing in the wonderful ocean air, we took off our shoes and socks to wade in the shallow surf. While my companion searched for Mediterranean pebbles, I reveled in the peaceful surroundings and praised the Lord for the privilege of being a missionary to Morocco.

The Mission Begins

A hundred years ago, the roots of my mission, Gospel Missionary Union, spread across the Atlantic Ocean and entwined the heart of Morocco. Gibraltar, Tangier and El Ksar were key steppingstones to the target area, central Morocco. At great sacrifice, missionaries of old had opened the door and laid the foundation for the full and satisfying missions career my colleagues and I had.

In the 1800s, the Young Men's Christian Association was a lively parachurch organization with a heart for evangelism. The 1888 YMCA convention in Abilene, Kansas, is considered the birthplace of GMU and other missions.

George S. Fisher, a former customs official and YMCA's first Kansas State Secretary, strode down the aisle to open that convention with powerful gospel singing. Stirred with emotion, the convention's delegates joined in with enthusiasm, "Am I a soldier of the cross, a follower of the Lamb? / And shall I fear to own His cause, or blush to speak His name?" During the five days of the Abilene Convention, attended by hundreds of men, conference organizers continually presented the need of heathen lands "where Christ is not named" to the delegates. They began with prayer at daybreak, met in session all day and continued far into each night.

The Spirit of God was at work. At dawn the final morning, after an all–night prayer and worship session, some delegates still knelt, singing softly, "I'll go where you want me to go, dear Lord / I'll be what you want me to be." Two years later, nine of these men sailed to Sierra Leone; within a short time, five of them had died.

Fisher and his associates were deeply stirred. The deaths of these five young men inspired others to enter missionary work. However, the YMCA International Committee called the deaths "the result of unbounded zeal for the cause, precious lives lost that ordinary caution might have saved." To stay with YMCA, George Fisher would have to temper his zeal. However, if he chose to leave this respected organization, he could expect further criticism. He understood that a break in fellowship and a lack of funds might hamper his ministry, which was so effective under the umbrella of YMCA.

The burden for foreign missions that God had placed on Fisher's heart would not go away. He felt compelled to pursue his calling. In January 1892, Fisher and several of his associates resigned from YMCA to set up a new, independent organization called the World's Gospel Union. Apparently the parting was peaceful. A note in the minutes of the International Committee of the YMCA stated simply that "the State continued to operate independently."

When fire destroyed the mission headquarters in Abilene in 1895, the organization moved to Kansas City, where they rented an empty YWCA building. Another party had gone to West Africa, and again, several died. Among them was Charles Helmick, who before leaving had quoted an earlier pioneer: "Though every step be over the grave of a missionary, yet the command of our Lord, 'Go ye into all the world,' must be carried out."

Pioneers to Morocco

In 1894, George Fisher's first band of missionaries set out for Morocco. The party included a one–armed preacher named Henry Hammer and Albert Nathan, a Jewish convert, with his wife, four small children and Hettie, their maid. *The Gospel Message*, the official magazine published by the mission, carried this note: "Henceforth let every reader stow away the Moroccan missionaries in one good, warm corner of the heart, or possibly the middle room would be a good place – just between the praying and the doing side." As the four adults and four children boarded the ship in New York Harbor, Henry Hammer, the preacher, exclaimed, "Lift up your eyes, Morocco, for a gleam of light is coming to you!"

Morocco was terribly in need of a gleam of light. On the coast, a certain amount of civilization might be found, but inland travel was perilous. The Arab conquerors had never subdued the Berbers, the original inhabitants of the land. With several strong Berber tribes constantly at war, the Arab king used barbaric methods to put down the tribes. It was not unusual to see the heads of conquered tribesmen hanging in the city square.

Slavery still existed, especially with the selling of women and children. Slave traders assembled their victims in the marketplace and sold them like cattle. The new slaves brought anywhere from forty to 200 dollars each, depending on their age, strength and beauty. Traders sold not only black slaves from south of the Sahara but also white women and children, captured from English and other European ships.

Christians, called *Nsara* (Nazarenes), were barely tolerated. Two British missions, The British and Foreign Bible Society and North Africa Mission, who opened work in Tangier, welcomed the American group. A year after the first American missionaries settled in Morocco, a second party set out: a wealthy man named Rockafellar, with his wife and little daughter Nellie, a young woman named Martha Richards (who married Henry Hammer) and Clinton Reed.

After a brief period of language study in Tangier, the group left to open a mission station in the ancient inland city of Meknes. Authorities there refused to grant the new missionaries housing in the Muslim sector of town. They finally found a place to live in the low-lying, unsanitary Jewish quarter, called the *mellah* (salt). The Jews had the unsavory job of preserving the heads hung in the city gates by salting them, which is how their neighborhood got its name. The Jewish quarter carries the same title to this day. Early GMU missionaries, though praying for a more suitable place to live, accepted this lowly place with humility and grace, tolerating it as long as their health held out.

Mission archives contain an article titled "A Queer Band of Religious Enthusiasts in Kansas City," which appeared in the *New Orleans Picayune* newspaper, January 31, 1897:

> Young men and women in Kansas City are giving up positions in stores and offices to join a remarkable institution, which does nothing except praise God and preach the gospel, which relies on the literal sending of food and clothing for its members by divine providence, says the *Kansas City Star*. Yesterday was wash day, and all the men joined in the work of washing the linen of the institution. The chief item of food is bread. . . . At various times the members of the "Gospel Union," as it is called, start out for South America or Africa, penniless and without knowing the language, to preach the gospel.

Although very human, as shown by the writings they left behind, the young missionaries were exceptional saints of God. They were great scholars and amazing linguists, quickly becoming adept at both European and Middle Eastern languages. They learned to read and write colloquial Arabic and Shilha, among the most difficult languages in the world. In a short time, they translated major portions of the New Testament. The hymns they translated echoed throughout Morocco for seventy–five years and still bless the hearts and strengthen the faith of believers.

The article in the *Picayune* newspaper expressed astonishment that Superintendent A.R. Perry (a banker before joining Gospel Missionary Union) "seemed to feel the utmost complacence about having two men land in Ecuador absolutely penniless to preach the gospel. 'God will take care of them,' he said with absolute confidence." When asked,

"Would you send out women that way?" Perry answered, "I see no reason, if they are called by God, why they should not go, just like the men."

That occasion soon arose. Single women began volunteering to go to far–off places, including Morocco. In 1901, Maude Cary, single and only twenty–three years old, went with a party sent to carry out the Great Commission in Morocco. She had signed on for life, expecting never to return home.

The Work Develops

For forty–five years GMU missionaries saturated large portions of central Morocco with the gospel. The women ministered in the coastal city of El Ksar, inland at Meknes, in the mountain town of Sefrou and occasionally in the great city of Fes. They visited in harems, preaching the gospel to women who seldom left their homes. They sold Scripture portions, held classes, spoke openly to large crowds, translated hymns and Scriptures and painstakingly checked other translators' work. During that period four young men, F.C. Enyart, Victor Swanson, Clinton Reed and George Reed, lived with Berber families, teaching, preaching and living out the gospel. Inland markets became their regular pulpits.

Bible translation was a priority. These young missionaries translated the four Gospels into Shilha and the entire New Testament into colloquial Arabic, the language of the street throughout Morocco.

The British and Foreign Bible Society had been established to publish and distribute Bibles and Scripture portions in various languages. Typesetting facilities were not available for the finished work, so the missionaries started looking for a scribe to prepare the final manuscript. Capable Muslim scribes could be found, but none were willing to copy the exact translation because it contained statements they considered blasphemous.

Using samples of writing done by the Sultan's scribe, Victor Swanson secretly practiced writing the beautifully flowing script, written from right to left, which calls for "every jot and tittle" to be exact. When satisfied, he presented a sample of his own handwriting to the group, not telling them it was his. Pleased with the work, they asked if the scribe would be willing to do the job. Swanson admitted it was his own handwriting. George Fisher appointed him to the task of painstakingly inscribing the entire New Testament.

The mission purchased property in the market town of Khemisset, which is between Casablanca and Meknes, and established stations in rented homes in Meknes and Sefrou. For all of their effort, though, they saw few converts. In time the missionaries aged, died or left the field because of illness. The solid foundation of talented, undaunted, energetic young missionaries making up the Morocco staff had dwindled to two – and they were women.

Chapter 2
I Join the Team

When World War II engulfed North Africa, Maude Cary and Signe Johnson were the only veteran missionaries left in Morocco. The founders of the mission had died, and one by one the other men had left the field for various reasons. The passing of time demanded some changing of the guard at the headquarters in Kansas City. J. Calvin Jones succeeded Fisher as president of the mission in 1929. Only one man remained in Morocco – a brilliant language student, a talented and dedicated missionary, a man who after two years on the field was beginning to direct the work.

Maude Cary returned from furlough in 1937 to resume her ministry, which, with George Christian Weiss at the helm, seemed very promising. While she was en route to Morocco, Jones, GMU's president, died of cancer. Mission leaders recalled Weiss to Kansas City to teach in the GMU Bible school and to represent GMU in churches and Bible colleges in the United States. Within a short time, he became the third president of the organization, leaving the GMU work in Morocco in the hands of Miss Cary and Miss Johnson.

Besieged by War

Charles Fraser-Smith, an independent agricultural missionary from England, owned a house next door to the GMU station in Khemisset, as well as 250 acres of farmland two and a half miles from town. He registered the property under the name "Sunset Farm."

Fraser-Smith was about to start an orphanage on the farm when World War II interrupted those plans. On June 14, 1940, Paris fell to the Germans; a new French government signed an armistice with Italy. The terms of the agreement included French withdrawal from all its colonies. Fraser-Smith knew the French Governor-General of Morocco, a Fascist sympathizer, was likely to help the German and Italian cause. He made the agonizing decision to take his family back to England for the duration. On board their ship home were other British missionaries, leaving just before North Africa fell to the Germans.

The British missionaries, on their way home to England, and two young American ladies, GMU missionaries en route to Morocco, traveled safely through treacherous waters. Packs of German U–boats patrolled the seas, and the German Luftwaffe dominated the skies. In the Mediterranean the Germans held most of the bases for controlling traffic at sea. When Italy declared war on Great Britain and her allies on June 10, 1940, it had 200,000 troops in Libya and 1,500 aircraft. Britain had fewer than 400 aircraft in the whole Middle East to defend Gibraltar, the strategic island of Malta, the Suez Canal and the Sudan.

Enemy forces soon occupied Morocco. The North African campaign escalated. European countries fought against each other on foreign soil, bombing the cities, devastating the countryside and destroying the livelihood of the innocent and uninvolved North African people.

In Morocco, four missionary women began their wartime vigil at Meknes, living together in Derb Skat so Ellen Doran and Emmagene Coats, the new missionaries, could learn the language. Later they spread out to keep the Sefrou and Khemisset stations open.

Because of the German occupation of Morocco, the missionaries couldn't obtain funds from America. Even if they had money, there was little to buy because foreign trade was halted and foreign colonists – the merchants and businessmen in the country – had fled. German antiaircraft guns were set up at the village hospital near the mission station in Khemisset, uncomfortably close for American citizens who could have been captured and imprisoned.

Liberation for Morocco came when General Dwight D. Eisenhower commanded an Allied offensive from Gibraltar under the code name "Torch." Eisenhower and his troops struck Algeria and Morocco, clearing the northern coast of

Africa, opening the Mediterranean Sea and establishing a North African base from which to strike Italy. The "free" French, a strong element bitterly opposed to the Vichy government that had sold itself to the Nazis, supported the Allied forces from inside North Africa.

At 4:00 a.m. November 8, 1942, U.S. forces landed at three ports around Casablanca and fought their way inland. Finally, on November 10, 1942, the resident general of Morocco requested and obtained orders from his superior in Algiers to surrender. The years of terror, indignity and deprivation were over. When the liberating American troops rolled through town, the missionary ladies joined the crowd of thin, ragged Moroccans along the highway and shed tears of joy.

Coming to Him

I am amazed at the way God picks His workers, many from the most unlikely places. I was born in Sleepy Eye, Minnesota, on a cold, stormy day, March 6, 1917. My parents had moved to Minnesota from Illinois, and this, their first winter there, was among the hardest our area ever experienced. A few days after I was born, my father had to dig a tunnel through the snowdrift between the house and the barn to reach the cows.

My parents did not go to church, and I was eleven years old before I entered a church for the first time. I was so ignorant of Christianity, I didn't even know the New Testament was part of the Bible. After we had moved to the town of St. James in southwestern Minnesota, a missionary from the American Sunday School Union called at our home when I was sixteen years old. He wanted to ask permission to open a Sunday school in our local schoolhouse. My father, who was on the school board, said he was in favor if the others all agreed.

I paid no attention to the caller and didn't go with my parents to the opening meeting at the school that evening. My mother volunteered my services to become secretary and treasurer of the Sunday school. Humiliated and angry, I went the first Sunday to refuse the position. To my surprise, I liked it. And for the first time, I heard the gospel.

Our Sunday school teacher came each week with his wife and mother to teach the classes. After a few weeks they invited a pastor they knew to hold a meeting during the Sunday school hour. The pastor spoke on "the Word," and his message deeply impressed me. As I started to leave, someone stopped me and took me to meet the pastor. I expressed my delight in the Word and my desire for more meaning in my life. They showed me many verses from the Bible explaining my need. I wanted to find these verses on my own, but I was too bashful to ask. When they showed me a verse that read, "Him that cometh to me I will in no wise cast out" (John 6:37 KJV), I peeked at the corner of the page and saw "John 6." I wanted to find the page with that word and number in the corner in a Bible at home.

That day, I became a member of God's family. I thanked Him for the miracle I knew He had done in me. Everything in my life changed from that day on.

But I couldn't forget John 6. Every moment I had the next day, starting with Genesis, I turned page after page looking for John 6. By evening I had found it, and I read it for myself.

My heart was hungry for more knowledge of the Bible, and I treasured the moments I could spend with my mentor, the Sunday school teacher, learning new spiritual truths. Whenever I went to his store to get groceries, he always pulled out his New Testament and gave me a special bit of new knowledge. I was not only delighted to receive the Word of God, but it impressed me that this businessman carried part of the Bible with him every day.

My ignorance of the Word as a teenager helped me as a missionary because I could relate to the Moroccans' questions and I knew what would help them most. Especially as I studied Hebrews, I could see so clearly that Christ's blood shed to forgive my sins gave my new, eternal life much meaning. Because Hebrews is my favorite book of the Bible, I taught it with enthusiasm. It's no wonder one of our believers in

Morocco said that his favorite book of the Bible was Hebrews also.

Totally occupied with my new relationship with God, I soon lost many of my friends. My mother worried about this. She learned about Bible college from a young couple who came to help in Vacation Bible School and stayed in our home. When I expressed a desire to attend Northwestern Bible School in Minneapolis, Minnesota, she willingly let me go.

Student life in the late 1930s was a struggle. Most of us financed our way through college by working in private homes for room, board and a stipend. Once I didn't have enough money for carfare to return home on the streetcar. I didn't know what I would say to the conductor, but as the streetcar approached, I walked out to board. As I got on, I saw at my feet the token I needed to pay my fare. I picked it up, slipped it into the coin box and arrived at work on time.

Another time I had no hose to wear (wearing hose was required) and no money. I had decided to give all of my wages to missions, not even saving enough for carfare for the week. When I returned to work, my employer told me I could have a free ride to and from school the following week. She also gave me three pair of hose, although I was not aware that she knew my need. Through financial hardship I learned to trust the Lord for daily needs, which prepared me for my future life as a missionary.

Practical work also helped me prepare for Morocco. I began teaching a class in a small mission in Minneapolis. During the summer I went with other students to various small towns in Minnesota to teach Vacation Bible Schools. We had one unusual experience in a VBS when several twelve- and thirteen-year-old children gave their lives to the Lord. They organized a prayer group that continued to meet for several years. Their parents often heard them praying and were amazed at their understanding of spiritual ideas and at the things they requested in their prayers.

The Call to Missions

I met a missionary for the first time at a conference in Iowa. Later, while in college, I began to get acquainted with missionaries who frequently spoke in chapel services. One of them was a man who served at a boy's home in Tangier, Morocco. He showed us pictures of the boys in their *jelabas* (long robes worn by both men and women) and red *fezzes* (round, box-like hats with black tassels). The missionary was the son–in–law of Herbert P. Elson, an American missionary who went to Morocco under GMU in 1896. Elson started an orphanage and school after he found a little, ragged, homeless boy on his doorstep. The child told him he had come to stay in his home. This story sparked a love in my heart for the people of Morocco.

In preparation for a report, I read a book on missions where I learned Morocco was among the most spiritually neglected countries. It was also one of the hardest places in the world to spread the gospel. This challenged me, and I offered myself to contribute money and pray for this country. I finished my report, drew a map of Africa and circled the country of Morocco. I named it "my country."

The next morning on the way to the chapel service, I submitted my report to the missions department. When I arrived at the chapel, I learned the speakers were missionaries to Morocco. Thus I met G. Christian Weiss, and his speech about the great need in that country challenged me.

I offered myself not only to give and pray but to go. I applied to GMU and they invited me to go to Kansas City as a candidate in 1941. Still, I wondered how God could use a little, bashful girl like me to work in one of the most difficult places in the world.

Since the war hindered the mission from sending anyone to Morocco, I went back to Northwestern, where I studied Greek, Spanish and typing. My first assignment after completing my postgraduate work at Northwestern was in the country village of Tightwad, Missouri, where for two years I worked with godly missionaries. We visited in homes, held

Sunday school and church meetings in various places and taught weekly Bible classes in the public schools. Sometimes we walked ten miles to and from a school. After meetings at night, we walked home on lonely country roads, listening to dogs and foxes racing across the fields.

From Tightwad I went to a GMU ministry in Topeka, Kansas. Not many children were attending classes, so I went into the street and gathered neighborhood children. We also asked teachers to announce in the schools that we had children's Bible classes, and we soon filled the classroom. I held the same types of classes near other Topeka schools.

While in Topeka, I enrolled in a French class at a local university. This introduced me to one of the foreign languages I would need in the multilingual country of Morocco.

At last, the war was over. Several prospective missionaries applied for visas at the same time. While waiting for a reply from the immigration office in Chicago, I moved to the mission headquarters in Kansas City. My name was accidentally omitted from the first visa list that came through. One party sailed to Morocco, while I stayed behind.

Nine long months went by before we received a response from Chicago, and by that time, discouragement had dwindled the group that remained. I was the only one still planning to go. The telegraph finally arrived, but my name was missing again. Another telegram assured me that the French government of Morocco had accepted my application. The Lord supplied funds through the Topeka Bible Church, where I had been attending. They offered to take on my full support: twenty-five dollars a month.

On to Morocco!

I traveled by train to Virginia, where I spent Christmas with friends, and then to New York City, where Maude Cary was waiting for me. She had been in the United States for surgery and hoped to take several workers back with her to Morocco – she had prayed for ten men. She had only me, but I was excited and ready to go.

Miss Cary had booked a place on a freighter, but they had room for only one passenger. We waited in New York several days, praying for a boat with space for two so we could travel together. At last we learned of a freighter ready to sail to Casablanca, with space for both of us. I was happy, relieved and thankful to God because I didn't want to travel alone. On January 19, 1946, we sailed out of New York Harbor, on our way to Casablanca.

The first week on board the ship the sea was rough. The second week was calmer, and the sea was beautiful. Having nothing to do but study French, I became bored. The freighter carried only twelve passengers on board. They became my friends. I shared the gospel with the passengers, officers and crew.

On February 2, 1946, we finally arrived in Casablanca. The day was perfect: calm, blue and mild, the kind of showcase winter weather that draws tourists to the Mediterranean region. My first glimpse of that beautiful port was the wreckage of the ships sunk during the war. That the Moroccan people had suffered intensely during the German occupation was readily apparent.

Arriving at the dock was an incredible experience. We could hardly stand in the press of the crowd. I shall never forget my first look at my chosen people – a welcoming committee of noisy, ragged Arab porters competing for our baggage, not at all what I had imagined from written accounts of colorful people in baggy yellow pants and picturesque red *fezzes*. I had been transported to a new world – with amazing new sights, strange new sounds and brand-new smells.

I didn't have time to ponder, though. Strangers grabbed our luggage and carried it first to customs and then to the train depot. I had my first ride in a *calàche*, a little one-horse carriage. And when the wheel broke, I was grateful none of my friends back home were there to see me clumsily arise from the heap.

Chapter 3
Derb Skat: So This Is Home!

Casablanca was a major Atlantic seaport on the northwest coast of Morocco. Meknes, our destination, was several hours inland, so we boarded a train for the last stretch of our journey. When the train pulled into the Meknes station, it was 2:00 a.m. and raining. We took a taxi – another horse–drawn carriage – from the station in the European section of Meknes to the *medina*, the ancient, walled–in Muslim sector of town.

It was not the storybook tourist ride I might have expected. I was nervous because of the late hour and uncomfortable because of the rain. Although I was excited to be so close to the home I had dreamed of for so long, the late–night arrival was more than I had bargained for. In the darkest hour before dawn, we stepped from the carriage into the heart of the sleeping city.

Although my senior missionary must have been tired, she was lighthearted. Bravely I marched along with her, but my heart almost stopped when we suddenly turned into a pitch–black alley. I was supposed to have a flashlight ready. Trembling, I reached into my bag and searched for it in vain. Then, as I was about to give up, my hand touched cold metal. Relieved, I switched the flashlight on, and we walked to the end of the alley.

I shuddered as the sound of the knocker echoed through the stillness of the night. While we waited for a response, I became keenly aware of other sounds around me. Water was running inside the walls on either side of us. I later discovered it was river water channeled through the homes for household purposes. For forty–three years, every time I heard that water running my mind flipped back to the terrifying night of my arrival.

Maude Cary looked up as she waited. I flashed the light up the wall and saw a tiny window far above the door. A light came on. Finally we saw a head appear and a confident voice called out, "*Ash-koon?* (Who is there?)" When the missionary above us discovered who we were, she pulled a rope and the center of the huge, heavy door swung open. We stepped into a dark passageway leading to a lighted court, firmly closing the door behind us. Signe Johnson, living alone in the big house at the time, rushed down the stairs to enfold us into her welcoming arms.

Learning About My New Home

Even in daylight, stepping through the gate into the ancient city for the first time was an awesome experience. The whitewashed walls of centuries–old, windowless stone houses towered above the main thoroughfare, creating a walled–in cobblestone street. The house we lived in was at the end of a narrow, dead–end alley, or *derb*, jutting off the main street. An upstairs room bridged one section of the alley, almost creating a tunnel. There were four huge entry doors in the *derb*. From the outside the four houses looked alike, but once inside we found obvious differences. Two doors led to elaborate homes, the third to a huge house shared by several families.

The fourth door was the one at the end of the alley that we had entered the night before. It was our "front door" and the only entrance to the house. The kitchen and main living quarters were on the second floor. We could look out of what we called our "*ashkoon* window" to see who was there. Earlier missionaries had invented a clever device that enabled us to open the door from the second story by pulling a rope through a pipe between the floors. It was an effective security measure, allowing us to open the door only to people we knew and trusted.

The massive entry door to our house, Derb Skat, was nine feet high and five feet wide. It contained a smaller door in the decorative arch design so common in the Mideast. We used the small door most of the time. Most adults had to stoop to enter. Once inside, the hallway led them to a spacious tiled court lit by an opening in the roof, forty or fifty feet above the court. A modern entrance eventually replaced the ancient front door. However, the dark, narrow *derb* leading to our house didn't change at all over the years.

Surrounding the court, the second floor had a five-foot balcony supported by four great columns. A sturdy railing allowed a person to lean over and watch the activity in the court below. The balcony served as a hallway to the upstairs rooms, which also had the elaborately carved wooden doors with the smaller doors for entry. The heavy large doors ran on an axle dating back to the Roman era. Such doors have been found in Roman ruins near Meknes and elsewhere in North Africa.

Morocco (Arabic for "The Land Farthest West") lies at the opposite end of the Mediterranean Sea from Palestine. It is at least 4,000 miles west of Arabia, but Middle Eastern architecture and customs prevail. Many Bible verses came alive for me almost immediately upon entering the country. The small doors within the larger ones, for example – or small arches within the gigantic gates in the city walls – are called "the eye of the needle." (Jesus referred to them in Matthew 19:24 when He said, "It is easier for a camel to go through the eye of a needle than for a rich man to enter the kingdom of God.") A loaded camel would have difficulty squeezing through the small archway (and it's tough, although possible, for a rich person to surrender to Christ).

Above the second floor of Derb Skat was a flat roof with a skylight opening over the court, covered by iron grill work to keep thieves out of the court. A screen covered the skylight to keep the birds out. None of this prevented the rain from drenching us, however, and during the rainy season we carried an umbrella to move from room to room. A drain in the floor of the court carried away excess water.

The mission occupied the house forty years before someone found a way to cover the opening while keeping the advantages of light and fresh air. Bob Schneider built a wooden frame over the skylight, covered it with tin roofing, and built windows that could be opened and closed to let in light and air. He often said, "We are entitled to a roof over our heads."

Rooftops are the women's domain, a safe place where they can be outdoors, do the laundry, bathe, relax with embroidery and gossip with other women on adjoining rooftops. Men are not allowed to look down on a neighbor's roof. No one could look down on ours, at any rate. Our house loomed far above any others around us, and our rooftop walls were very high. Missionaries living at Derb Skat got into trouble once, though. Because the rooms were windowless, one group of missionaries decided to build a window high up on the twenty-foot wall. Unfortunately, it overlooked someone's roof. Soon neighbors came over to complain, asking the missionaries to close the window. It is boarded up to this day.

In one corner of our roof, there was a small room where I made my home during the first years of my life in Morocco. We called it "the prophet's chamber" because it reminded us of the room the Shunammite woman prepared for the prophet Elisha in 2 Kings 4. The room was not very big, holding only a narrow bed, a small wardrobe and a stand with a lamp on it. I had to climb fifty-three stairs from the court to my quarters, but the roof, and its privacy, was just steps away from my room.

The walls of Derb Skat, which separated our house from the neighbors, were three feet thick. Morocco is very hot for several months each year, but Derb Skat, particularly the ground level, stayed delightfully cool throughout the most scorching summer months. Country Berbers, some of whom had known the early missionaries, stopped by over the noon hour for tea, a snack and a siesta when they were in town. Noontime naps are common in North Africa. Shops close for two to three hours, and activity in the street slows to a snail's pace. Any occasion that brought people into our home provided an opportunity for either evangelism or discipleship training. We welcomed the siesta group whenever they came.

A doorbell eventually replaced the knocker on the front door, and it rang constantly. I loved people, so it was music to my ears. When I was on the lower floor, I made a dash to the door; if I was upstairs, I ran to the *ashkoon* window to see who was standing at the door below. It might have been an individual I was praying for, maybe someone wanting to know the way of salvation. It could have been someone in deep emotional trouble, or someone who wanted prayer or counseling or had questions about their new faith. My co-workers teased me about the times I put things in the oven upstairs and went to the court below to deal with some spiritual need. More often than not, the food looked like charcoal when I returned.

Perhaps it was the tradition brought from America by our pioneer missionaries, or possibly it was the British influence. Whatever the case, we were very formal in front of the Moroccans, always "Miss Davis," "Miss Janz," "Mr. Schneider" or "Mr. Yoder," or the French "Monsieur," "Madame" or "Mademoiselle." This custom seemed senseless to me. Why should I call my elders by their first name while expecting them to address me as "Miss Davis?" Moreover, with the young people and children always tugging my sleeve for attention or calling to me in the street, it sounded more like "Muss–tah–vis."

I shared a horse–drawn carriage taxi with a woman one day as I returned home from the new part of town. As we rolled down the hill, she, being very friendly, asked what my name was. I said, "Miss Davis."

"Really!" she exclaimed. "That's just like my husband, Mustapha."

I finally chose the name "Liela," because it sounded like "Ila" and was a Moroccan name commonly known to all. My name worries ended that day. From then on I heard a thousand voices, young and old, cry, "Liela!" "Liela!" It was a sweet sound to me.

Moroccan winters are bitterly cold. Snow remains on the higher altitudes of the Atlas Mountains year–round. Meknes sits on the lower, fertile plains, where hard, driving rains drench the city streets for weeks on end. The same stone and tile that make summers comfortable turn Derb Skat and houses like it into unbearably frigid chambers in the winter. We layered on many sweaters and warm socks to keep warm. It was impossible to heat the whole house, so each occupant had to work out some kind of portable heating system. Wood stoves and kerosene heaters were two possible choices. Moroccans used charcoal for cooking and for warming their hands. They put on extra clothing as well and, like us, were uncomfortable when the room got too warm.

In February 1960 a terrible earthquake destroyed the coastal city of Agadir. Eleven thousand people died, some from starvation under tons of rubble while waiting to be rescued. This incident was fresh in my mind when one night, to my horror, I heard a roar, like a noisy motor going through my room. Then–new missionaries Gordon and Daphne McRostie and their children lived with me. I lived on the lower floor, while the family slept on the second floor. Stones began to creak and crackle along the walls. I recognized it as an earthquake; what should I do? I didn't want to be buried alive!

All I could think of was to pray that a stone would fall on my head and kill me quickly! Then, remembering the two babies upstairs, I jumped up, ran into the court and looked up. Two very frantic parents were leaning over the rail, not knowing what to do.

The Lord still had a purpose for us on earth. The foundation quit rocking and no damage was done. Mothers with little children who lived at Derb Skat underwent some special trials, but probably none quite as terrifying as the night the earth shook beneath Derb Skat.

The Center of our Ministry

The Derb Skat house was built in the sixteenth century as a mansion for a princess. When the princess died, the house became the property of the king. Since he owed money to a member of his royal family living in Meknes, he gave him the house to repay the debt. Early missionaries rented the house and passed the lease on to their successors. Decorating by the missionaries, of course, depended on budget and personal taste, and in Morocco the contrast between rich and poor is well defined. Missionaries in Morocco formed a new "middle class." They were much richer than the poor, who often had nothing, but much poorer than the rich, whose homes and wearing apparel bordered on the exquisite and luxurious. Missionaries moving to Derb Skat inherited ancient secondhand furnishings and added their personal touch to make it home.

Morocco's mosaic tile with intricate geometric patterns in vivid colors has made it famous. The floor and walls in Derb Skat boasted this easy-care tile – cool and comfortable in summer, icy during winter. I visited many beautiful homes with similar designs. Overstuffed couches upholstered in rich velour, with richly embroidered or velour pillows on which to recline, filled the Moroccans' rooms. The wealthy had lovely low tables with an inlaid pearl design, shining brass trays, sparkling copper teakettles and thick woolen rugs deftly woven by creative women and children.

The imagination was seldom disappointed when stepping through the great doors of a wealthy home. Only the occupants' gracious hospitality and good food surpassed the luxury, comfort and beauty of the homes. Derb Skat hostesses found a middle ground where both rich and poor could feel welcome. In this atmosphere visitors listened to the message of the gospel – frequently or for the first time.

Our house saw many changes through the years. Before my time, some missionaries built shafts at the end of the narrow, thirty-foot-long rooms to let in more outside light. At best, the bathroom facilities of early North African city homes consisted of a tiled hole in the ground with a sewer connected to the underground river. One era of missionaries built a European-style bathroom in Derb Skat, conveniently located in a hall between the first and second floor. City water was piped into the kitchen, which had a double sink and cupboards.

Missionaries came and went, and they changed the huge rooms to meet their needs. Walls were built and torn down, door openings were cut and closed up again. Once while I shared the house with another single woman, we decided to tear down a half wall separating a small bedroom from the living room so we could have one large room. With an ax and a heavy hammer we struck the wall. It came tumbling down. We used the bricks to close a doorway from the bedroom to the stairway and built a brick bookshelf on one side of the expanded living room.

Downstairs we installed a swinging door between the entry hall and the court. When the outside door was open, strangers in the *derb* could see into the court. It worried me, especially during our Bible conferences, that an enemy of the gospel might come to the door and see what was going on. It was unlawful for Muslims to convert to Christianity, so I didn't want a passerby to report our meetings to the police. The hallway door was a security measure to protect believers.

As the years passed, many missionaries stretched a net across the court to play volleyball. Missionary children rode their bikes there and played with wagons and balls. We held large Christian conferences there every year, and we used this ample space for Vacation Bible Schools, retreats, parties and weddings.

Derb Skat was a spacious, spectacular and strategic house, and I loved the place that became home to me in Morocco. The decades of prayer by the early missionaries and saints back home were answered in the eighty–plus years GMU missionaries occupied the house. The gospel was faithfully explained, prayers were offered and answered, children learned the Word of God, battles were fought and won in our own spiritual lives, and many souls were brought into the Kingdom of God between those heavy stone walls.

Chapter 4

A Tour of the Town

As a new missionary I went on a tour of Meknes. My fellow missionaries assured me it would not take long to feel at home in this maze of activity. In no time at all, I was orienting new missionaries and entertaining guests by showing off our town.

The first stop was generally the public oven, easy to find thanks to the smell of fresh bread that filled the air. Moroccan women baked fresh bread every day, assigning someone from the household to carry the bread to the oven and later to pick it up. Dozens of bread boards, about two feet in length, lined the "lobby," each stacked with two, six or even more round, flat loaves of unbaked, rising bread.

The owner of the oven didn't need any reminders of whose bread belonged to whom. He knew the identity of the owners by the scarves that covered the dough or the designs on the dough made with a fork. By midmorning, the fire at the public oven was hot. The oven operator picked up the loaves with a long-handled shovel and placed them on the oven floor beside the fire. With the same shovel he turned them over at precisely the right time. He kept a pile of wood and branches nearby to feed the fire.

The public bathhouse was next to the public oven, since the heat used for baking kept the rooms and water in the bathhouse hot as well. Women gathered there and spent the whole afternoon soaking in the burning steam, scrubbing each other with smooth stones and catching up on the latest gossip. The bathhouse had separate hours for men. Small children went with their mothers into the bath.

When customers entered the bathhouse, an attendant took their payment, handed them a basket and guarded their clothes until they were done. The next room was steamy but tolerable. The women sat on the floor for an hour or two before their bath to get used to the heat and darkness and, after they had finished, to cool off before leaving to dress. There they sipped sodas, peeled oranges, nursed their babies, rubbed their arms and legs with a pumice stone and talked.

The third steam room was so hot it all but took your breath away. Long hair, henna and orange peels floated past in the sloshing water in both rooms, clogging the drain. Many women sat for hours in the hottest room before they began to scrub themselves.

Some customers brought beautiful, silver pails with them, but most used wooden buckets furnished by the bath house. Fights often broke out over who got the bucket and for other major or minor reasons. With some women getting hit by buckets and others slipping and falling on the soapy floors, a few fainting from the long exposure to heat and some developing migraines, they came out of the bath looking as if they had gone through a war.

The city of Meknes boasts several tourist attractions, including an underground prison built by European slaves captured by the Barbary pirates. This huge and gruesome prison extends fourteen kilometers one direction and seven in the other. Part of the prison is boarded up because tourists sometimes got lost in the maze of underground passageways.

One had to crouch under an arch to enter the area where prisoners, hung by their hands with their feet in stocks, awaited death. The ground was often soggy and full of water holes. Human bones protruded from the walls of the ruins. When the slaves tired or completed their work they were thrown into the mortar to a horrible death.

Someone in one tour of Meknes saw a snake and jumped into action to kill it. The guard halted him, informing us that no animal could be killed in the area because it was the burial site of a "saint," Moulay Ishmael.

Meknes has a colorful past, its recorded history reaching back to the establishment of the Roman city, Volubilis, near the time of Christ. The prison, however, and the miles of wide stone walls were the work of Moulay Ishmael, "the Bloodthirsty." His seventeenth–century reign of terror lasted fifty-five years and united the kingdom, principally through the establishment of a black bodyguard of slaves from the south. The king's bodyguard maintained control in the then-capital city of Meknes and in forts called kasbahs that Ishmael built throughout Morocco. The descendants of these men fulfill the same duties today. Ishmael's harem supposedly rivaled Solomon's.

During times of siege, when Berbers from the countryside were attacking, the Arabs relied on an immense ancient granary that stored their grain and water. Behind this building the king kept thousands of horses in his stables.

Moulay Ishmael built the immense stone walls around Meknes, including a great wall that today goes nowhere. With ample slave labor available, he had planned to build a walled street all the way to Marrakech, hundreds of miles away.

The tomb of Moulay Ishmael and his sons is huge. A large fountain with running water occupies the first room, where people planning to pray can perform their ablutions. The next room is completely empty, as is a lower room, where one removes his shoes before entering the holiest room containing the three tombs. Beautifully carved and painted doors line the inner rooms, which are closed to the public.

Our tour always circled the *medina*, bringing us to our "shopping mall," a street called Khoub Essouk. Hundreds of little shops lined the narrow street. Grass mats covered the market to protect the shoppers from the hot sun in summer and the heavy rains in winter. Shops were cubbyholes side by side, and their wares were as varied as life itself: modern and traditional clothing; European shoes and traditional leather scuffs; specialty shops carrying silver, brass, wood, Moroccan-made rugs and leather bags, purses and billfolds – a fabulous display of the finest in Moroccan-made crafts.

Women crowded into the gold shops. They saw the eighteen-karat gold as an investment, which they protected by wearing it. There were gold rings, bracelets, belts and, for the brides, gold crowns.

The *svenge* shop was a favorite. *Svenge* is an unsweetened, raised doughnut, traditionally sold every morning for breakfast, although today it is sometimes served for afternoon tea.

Two men sat in the *svenge* shop, which was elevated to the height of the top of children's heads. In the middle of the shop was a tub of oil, kept hot by a man behind the shop who fed the fire underneath the tub. One man took the soft dough in his hands, made a ring with a quick move of his fingers and dropped the dough into the hot grease. The *svenge* rose in the boiling oil. With a metal tool he flipped it over. When it was browned to perfection, he lifted the big, bubbly doughnut out with a metal hook and laid it in a big pan to drain off the oil.

The second man in the shop took money from the customers, weighed the *svenge* and strung them on a fiber rope. Impatient children crowded around, waiting to get a *svenge* to eat on the way to school.

In time I became a familiar figure in the streets of the *medina*. All of the shopkeepers became my friends. I didn't have to bargain to get the right price. Many begged me to take my purchases and pay for them later to prove they trusted me. It became a good opportunity to witness for the Lord. Apparently I was part of the tour guide's repertoire, as well. I heard one tour guide saying, "And this is an evangelical missionary who lives among us!"

Admitting 'Infidels'

The mission's archives reveal that the struggle to obtain proper housing in Meknes went on for years. Courageously the pioneers traveled, preached in marketplaces and made friends of anyone who would have them, all in an attempt to establish a beachhead for missions in central Morocco. The government consistently denied the "infidels" housing in the *medina*. Frequently they evangelized in the region using a mission station in the city of Fes as their base.

The American ambassador finally refused to acknowledge a new royal regime until he received a promise that American missionaries could rent a house in a healthier and safer neighborhood of Meknes. In 1909, the Sultan granted the long–prayed–for permission. God had been at work preparing hearts for this favorable decision. Unwittingly, missionary Victor Swanson had sold a Bible to a dentist – the Sultan's dentist, as he learned much later. The dentist presented the Bible to the Sultan and returned to buy another for himself. Swanson and his colleagues rejoiced, believing that this event had softened the heart of the Sultan, leading to the answer to their prayer.

The house of the princess, 3 Derb Skat, was the Sultan's choice. The royal family rented it to the mission for the equivalent of $3.50 a month. Up through the time I lived there, the rent was raised only when the missionaries volunteered to raise it.

Laying the Foundation

Busy working women like the Derb Skat missionaries could hardly keep up such a huge house without hired help. One longtime maid in Meknes was a lady named El Allia. Her employment reached back to antiquity. Frank and Irene Enyart lived at Derb Skat periodically from 1909, when the missionaries obtained the house, until the 1930s, when they retired. One morning when Irene went to the market, a little boy begged to carry her vegetables home for her. As they talked, she mentioned she could use a woman to help with housework. He brought his mother, El Allia. Her husband had left her with two children to support. She was hired and served succeeding generations of missionaries.

El Allia turned out to be a good maid. Every day she came to the house she heard the gospel. Years afterward she confessed that it went in one ear and out the other. However, the lives of the missionaries made her feel that there was a power in the gospel the Muslims didn't have.

The missionaries caught El Allia stealing – not uncommon in Morocco – and after several offenses, let her go. For months at a time, no one would see her, but suddenly she would drop in and bring some friend or relative to hear the gospel. Often, in the only way a single mother could make a living, El Allia became a prostitute, sinking deeper into sin.

In 1939 the missionaries planned a Bible conference at Derb Skat, and they invited everyone they could think of to come. They spoke about El Allia and wished they knew where she was. The morning the meetings began, she appeared, saying she had had a dream.

In her dream she saw a wonderful place and a man she believed to be Christ, but she could not cross the river that separated them. He called to her to go to "headquarters" to find out what she should do. When she woke up, she was troubled. She thought "headquarters" must mean the house where the missionaries preached the gospel, so she came back, arriving just in time for the conference.

During the conference El Allia asked for prayer for salvation from her life of sin. From that time on she seemed to have a true desire to live for the Lord, though she often stumbled over her past sinful activities. She came back to work for the missionaries and heard the Word regularly again. She became a fixture at Derb Skat and was there when I arrived. When she asked for baptism, we were delighted to see her take that step because we believed her to be one of God's children.

Baptisms are rare in Muslim lands, but on May 2, 1947, we saw two dear Moroccan believers, El Allia and a young man named Jelali, take this step of obedience. GMU's John Barcus baptized the two, assisted by a French Foreign Legion veteran, Lebj (Leon) Feldman, a Jewish Christian who served as a missionary associate of GMU.

This was a rare and happy occasion, the first of many such intercultural delights. Clearly, four decades of difficult missionary work and faithful prayer support by folks back home were bringing results, and we looked to the future with enthusiasm and joy.

Chapter 5

Understanding the Competition

Before I went to Morocco, I read everything I could to learn about the country, the people and the religion. Once in Morocco, I soon felt the full effect of the people's religion and began to understand the large part it plays in their lives.

From the rooftop of Derb Skat we could count at least twenty minarets – tall mosque towers from which the call to prayer went out. A strange feeling swept over me the first time I stood on our roof at prayer time and watched the black–cloaked muezzin at the top of the mosque nearest our home.

"There he is!" I cried. Then a hush fell over us as a loud male voice began a call to prayer that would become as familiar to me as the chiming of a city clock: *"Allahu-Akbar! God is most great! God is most great! There is no god but God, and Muhammad is his Apostle!"*

Five times a day the call echoed from all the mosques across the *medina*. From among the crowds, almost unnoticed, shoppers, merchants from their shops, people from their homes, the faithful trekked to the nearest mosque to pray.

To understand Morocco and to effectively pray for and witness to Muslims, you need some insight into the religious fiber that weaves such a strong web, firmly binding into Islam all of society: family, education, citizenship, friendship, employment, holidays, customs, love, marriage, even childbirth. Everything important in life is tightly bound to the religion of the land.

Prayer: A Daily Ritual

The first prayer call of the day occurs at dawn before the sun comes up. At that hour, many devout Muslims put on their *jelabas* and wandered down to the nearest mosque.

The children quickly taught us about the ritual cleansing before prayer. Each mosque had a fountain in the center of the court, where the faithful stopped to wash their feet, hands and arms just over the elbows. The face, nose and throat had to be totally free from any corrupt matter.

Muslims often asked us how we washed ourselves before prayer. I always replied that we must cleanse our hearts from any sin before we can approach God, and I quoted Psalm 24:3–4, "Who may ascend the hill of the LORD? Who may stand in his holy place? He who has clean hands and a pure heart, who does not lift up his soul to an idol or swear by what is false."

Moroccan Muslims always face east, praying toward the Kaaba, the center of worship in Mecca, Saudi Arabia. Muslims on the other side of Mecca face west. When Muslims asked us which way we faced when we prayed, we said, "We face God."

Muslims believe they can trust a man who goes to prayer. But we've seen that this isn't always true. They always remove their shoes before they enter the mosque. Rows of shoes of every kind and make are placed side by side at the entrance. There is no guarantee they will still be there when the owner returns. For safety's sake, many take their shoes with them, tucked under their arms.

People can say their prayers in the street, in an open field, at home or wherever they are when the prayer call goes out. Devout workmen stop wherever they are working to pray. It is probably fair to say that most Muslim women do not pray; they are not allowed in the main area of the mosque. Even women who staunchly defend Islam and seem fanatical regard religion as a male concern.

Some women do pray, however. When we were visiting with them, they occasionally went to another room in the house or simply prostrated themselves by our feet during a visit or a party. Men and women alike wear *serwelle*, an undergarment much like a mid–calf skirt sewn shut across the hemline, allowing a few inches to insert the legs. While working, women tie their beautiful long dresses around their waists to protect them, making the *serwelle* the common, comfortable garb. Women often remove their *serwelle* before they pray because undergarments are considered ceremonially unclean.

Mosques are places of worship where the faithful gather for daily prayers. The Muslim holy day, which parallels the Jewish Sabbath and Christian day of rest, is Friday. (Muslim shops closed Fridays, Jewish shops closed Saturdays, and European or Christian shops closed Sundays – a bit of survival information a new missionary needed to remember.) A sermon could be heard at the mosque on Fridays.

Actually, the Muslim prayer could be termed "worship." There are no petitions or requests in it. It is a learned prayer filled with expressions of praise and adoration to Allah (the Arabic name for God). They always repeat the first chapter of the Qur'an (or Koran, the Muslims' holy book) and other memorized texts. And, of course, all Muslim prayers must be said in classical Arabic, which is taught by rote to young boys in the mosque schools.

Islam's Beginnings

Islam began with an individual convinced God had called him to be a spiritual reformer. Muhammad was born in A.D. 570 in Mecca, then the chief city of Arabia. His family belonged to a highly esteemed tribe called the Quraysh. Because he traveled with caravans of merchandise to Syria, he met Jews and Christians, from whom he learned a smattering of their religions. He worked for and then married a wealthy widow, which gave him a place of influence in Mecca.

The Arab descendants of Ishmael had become polytheistic – they worshiped many gods. A sect had arisen that opposed idolatry and declared its belief in one God, whom they called Allah. This sect sought to reestablish Abraham's religion.

The teaching intrigued Muhammad. He began to visit the leader of the sect, who, banished for preaching against idolatry in Mecca, was living in a cave. Finally, Muhammad decided to abandon idolatrous practices. He was forty years old when he claimed to have his first visit from the angel Gabriel.

The strange experiences continued, and they perplexed him. They seemed to occur when he was in a trance. This reassured him and his wife that he was receiving divine revelations. He began to preach that there was no god but Allah, and proclaimed himself to be Allah's apostle. Despite fierce persecution, his band of followers grew.

The Muslim calendar began in A.D. 622, the year Muhammad fled from Mecca to Medina, a town about 200 miles north of Mecca. At Medina he began to use force to propagate his message, enriching himself and his followers with the plunder they took from the people they conquered. His success as the head of this small army led him to enlarge his vision. He aspired to worldwide conquest for exterminating idolatry and establishing worship of Allah through himself, as Allah's apostle.

Muhammad's reign of terror lasted ten years, during which time he claimed the angel Gabriel dictated the Qur'an to him. He died in A.D. 632, leaving behind the caliphs, his successors, who carried on the "Holy War" with the battle cry still heard today, "There is no god but Allah, and Muhammad is the Apostle of Allah!" The armies were possessed with a wild fanaticism for Allah and his Apostle and a thirst for conquest. Because they had no fear of death, they were invincible. They believed those who fell in battle went immediately to paradise.

The new religion swept west, conquering the eastern Roman Empire, Damascus, the Persian empire, Egypt, other countries of North Africa and Spain. The Muslims were turned back in France and then turned eastward in an eventual sweep of Malaysia and parts of the Philippines, with some converts in western China. Wherever they went, the cry was the same: "There is no god but Allah, and Muhammad is the apostle of Allah!" To this they added, "Witness to the Apostle or die by the sword!"

The Berbers never submitted to Arab rule, but those who survived the Arab invasion embraced Islam. From the tiniest child to dying old men and women, the forefinger of the right hand was raised toward Allah to symbolize the witness even when the words couldn't be spoken.

Our Christian lives, in sharp contrast to Europeans and American military personnel who came in large numbers after World War II, impressed the Muslims in Morocco. Islam forbids the drinking of alcoholic beverages. The French often drank wine instead of water; drunken American sailors could be seen around the navy base.

As in our "Christian" nation, few in their Muslim state followed the rules of the book. Dr. Paul Harrison, a missionary to Arabia, wrote that he had never known people "with such a transcendence of God to whom a belief seems to make so little difference in the common morality of life." Yet Christian ethics appealed to the Muslim. Moroccans praised us for being good people, "so good that if only you would witness to the Apostle, you would surely get into heaven."

Religious Practices

The creed (*shahadah*), which is the witness to Allah and his Apostle Muhammad, is the only absolute requirement to become a Muslim. Prayer (*salat*) is practiced regularly only by the very devout. The giving of alms (*zakat*), the Ramadan fast (*sawm*) and the pilgrimage to Mecca (*hajj*) make up the remainder of the five pillars of Islam.

Zakat is a day when each Muslim is supposed to give one tenth of his income to the poor. Many shopkeepers close their shops on that day so they will not be forced to give coins to the multitude of beggars. Merchants who open their shops do so with a good amount of small change on hand. Usually, businessmen will give alms to needy members of their families. However, the beggars who sit along the street all year receive coins from almost every passerby.

Zakat is the children's "Christmas," the day they receive toys. The poorer the people, the cheaper the toys. Some don't even last through the day. On the other hand, wealthier people buy expensive toys and put them on a shelf to look at but not to touch. The evening before *zakat*, children build fires and delight in jumping over them without getting burned.

A person who never prays or gives alms is still considered a Muslim. However, one who breaks the fast of Ramadan (*sawm*) is no longer a Muslim and deserves prison, ostracism or even stoning. During the month-long fast, no one can smoke, eat, drink or take any kind of nourishment during daylight hours. Even the brushing of teeth or the use of perfume is forbidden. Neighbors may overlook someone's antisocial behavior, but it becomes everybody's business when they suspect someone of breaking the fast.

Average people take Ramadan very seriously. A young man with a degree from an American university and married to a European woman forbade his wife to make coffee in the morning for fear the neighbors would accuse him of breaking the fast. Some Christian families who did break the fast would cook their food at night so their hostile neighbors would not smell the aroma during the day. Sometimes they not only feared their neighbors but had a deep-seated fear that God might strike them with a calamity as punishment for eating. Breaking the fast is a serious offense.

I was eating an evening "breakfast" with friends one night during Ramadan. We all sat around the small table with *harera* (a special breakfast soup made of vegetables with a coriander base thickened by sourdough yeast) set out in dishes before us, ready to drink. Cigarettes were held, ready to light up, coffee and milk were poured. All we needed was to hear the sound of the siren announcing official sunset, and the family could dig in. Minutes felt like hours to the head of the house. Finally he announced that the siren had already sounded and that we, in our chattering, had not heard it. He picked up a date and had just plopped it in his mouth when he heard the awful sound. The siren. He spit out the food and looked around the table with shame, wondering how he could atone for this hasty mistake.

Hakim, a believer, worked at the airport, a job which provided his family with a good living. His vacation fell at the time of Ramadan. While visiting in his hometown, he came across an old friend, who was now a *cadi* – a religious judge and government official. The *cadi* asked Hakim if he kept the fast. "No, I don't," admitted Hakim. "Christians don't have a certain compulsory time to fast, but they fast voluntarily any time."

The *cadi* went immediately to the police station and accused his friend of eating during Ramadan. Hakim was arrested. During the trial his lawyer suggested that he claim illness as an excuse for eating during Ramadan. "I can't say that; I wasn't ill. I ate because I am a Christian," he said. He was convicted and sent to prison for six months.

While Hakim sat in prison, Christians in Morocco and all over the world prayed for him. Many sent money to help the family exist during his absence. This kindness touched the heart of his wife, encouraging her in her Christian faith. Generally if one is absent from work for more than two weeks, he loses his job. Through the prayers of God's people, Hakim got his job back when he was released from prison.

No one wants to go to prison; more than that, no one wants to bring shame on his family. Many believers insist they would be willing to suffer imprisonment but they couldn't endure the shame brought on the family.

Ramadan, for all its negative impact on the community, has some redeeming factors. What I liked best was that the whole family ate breakfast (at sunset) together. Bowls of *harera* break the fast, and the family enjoys many special foods such as dates, boiled eggs, honey cakes and *zamata* (a dish of wheat flour, sugar, nuts and sesame seeds). Everyone agrees that it costs more to live during Ramadan than at any other time of year. Custom seems to suggest they need richer nourishment to reward themselves for fasting.

After the evening breakfast, which is precisely at sunset, until the next meal, around midnight, everyone feels better. The cooks are busy, but everyone else is free to do as he pleases. During these hours we could have our Bible classes or worship services without risk of people accusing the participants of eating at our house. Some nights we played games with friends. Many city people took in movies, visited other homes, went for walks and, in later years, watched special television programs during that time. Stores are open all night but close in the morning until late afternoon.

The final meal of the night is at about 2:00 a.m., depending on the expected hour of sunrise. After a midnight meal, most people find it hard to awake, but they have to eat and drink before sunrise so they won't break the fast the next day. Days and nights are turned around. Children love Ramadan. Teachers are weary, classes are forgotten and teachers come late or not at all. Children ran the streets all night, and if they couldn't find anything else to do, they knocked on our door asking for a class.

For Christian believers, Ramadan is a stressful month. I often advised believers that Ramadan could neither help them nor hurt them, and that God was looking for a pure heart rather than an empty stomach. We expected them to show they had no confidence in the fast and withheld baptism until they had proven their sincerity by breaking the fast.

One sincere and well–loved woman who worked for the missionaries exemplified the unique stress placed on converts from Islam. Although she had broken the fast privately, she couldn't bring herself to partake of communion during Ramadan. A traumatic inner conflict tore her apart until later in the day when she settled the matter in her heart. Smiling through her tears, she accepted communion from the missionary in his home.

Not everyone makes the *hajj*, the coveted pilgrimage to Mecca. Those who do are given the title *hajji* or, for a woman, *hajja*. This fifth pillar of faith is not an obligation, and according to Islamic tradition, it is only for the wealthy and those whose health can endure the trip. When a son or daughter begins to work, the parents expect him or her to help save money for the *hajj*. Some pilgrims purchase merchandise in Mecca and sell it upon their return to help with expenses.

A woman under thirty–five years old cannot go on the pilgrimage alone. No one has to wonder what to wear on the pilgrimage. All pilgrims, rich or poor, are clad in the same simple attire of white cloth. The night before the pilgrim leaves on the trip the family holds a special farewell party. In this way, all relatives and friends can say goodbye, since it may be the last time they see him if he dies along the way. Those who die on the pilgrimage assuredly go to paradise.

Before air travel was common, pilgrims walked to Mecca, which could take a year or two. These days a flight of a few hours gets them to their destination. Some do not return, though. When the mother of one of our workers went on her pilgrimage, her son never heard from her again. Although her son searched for her, he never found her.

For those who do return, what a welcome home! Cars of relatives and friends, well decorated with ribbons and banners, meet the plane. The *hajji* or *hajja* is escorted by parade to his or her home, where a huge celebration is planned. New clothes await the celebrity just inside the door, and the party goes on.

I hadn't been in Morocco long when a neighbor returned from Mecca. At the gate where he got out of his son's car, his oldest wife waited for him. She carried her husband on her back through the busy street, into the alley where we lived and into their home. This feat assured her she would receive all the honor he did, as if she had taken the trip herself.

Islam is the state religion in Morocco, and we, although guests in the land, were teaching evangelical Christian beliefs, which the government interpreted as a challenge to the system. My life became a delicate balance between gentle acquiescence to the customs of the land and boldness to a faithful witness for Christ.

Chapter 6

Sacrifice, Sorcery and Satan

Studies of the Old Testament reveal that the ancient people of Israel celebrated special occasions throughout the year to commemorate various events or follow instructions established by God. These became great festivals – important holidays to them. Islam, too, has such holidays. *Id-al-Adha* (the Festival of Sacrifice) is the greatest holiday of all. Moroccans often called it *Aid-el-Kabir* (the Great Festival).

The Festival of Sacrifice is a commemoration of Abraham's taking Ishmael to the mountain to slay him. Islam maintains that God asked Abraham to sacrifice Ishmael rather than Isaac. In preparation for the feast, each household purchases a live sheep for the sacrifice. Since city–dwellers have no yards, the sheep are kept in the kitchen or court or on the roof. Each year before the feast, we could hear the bleating of the neighbors' sacrificial lambs and the pounding of spices.

Before the Great Festival, the children brim with excitement. They bring in all their friends to see the sheep and compare their sheep's horns with those of their friends' sheep. If their sheep's horns are larger, they dance with joy.

Everyone goes home for the Festival of Sacrifice. Taxis, buses and trains are crowded as each makes his way home to his family. Students who have been away at school, sons and daughters who live away from home, relatives from distant places, all crowd the highways.

Streets are wild the day before the feast. Last–minute buyers drag home their sheep, pushing them through the crowds in a wheelbarrow or cart or hoisting them into a taxi. Shoppers are out hunting for needed pots, pans and dishes, getting knives sharpened or selling unnecessary items for extra cash. You would think that with all the extra work the feast loads upon the women, one would be happy if her husband couldn't afford a sheep. But such a dilemma

53

embarrasses the whole family. Wives feel insulted and weep bitterly if their husbands can't provide sheep.

The morning of the feast, the men dress in their long, white robes and go out to an empty field to pray. Row after row of men stand, then fall to their knees in unison and finally touch the ground with their foreheads. Upon their return, the women have breakfast ready: sweet cakes and strong, sweetened coffee or sweet mint tea.

Around ten o'clock, the whole household, young and old, gathers to watch the butchering. With a flash of the knife, the throat is slashed. Blood runs across the floor, down the drains, into the sewers and then into the rivers and streams. Everything is red with blood the day millions of sheep are slaughtered.

I have seen women and girls wash their feet and legs with the blood of the slaughtered sheep. They believe it heals boils, sores or abrasions. In some homes, a bowl of blood is placed above the door, while others dab blood on the sides of the doorways. One dying woman begged to dip her fingers into the blood of the sacrifice. She lived to do that and then died.

Ritual fills the day, and most people know little of the purpose of the feast except that it is a great holiday, the custom of the land and a part of Islam.

The Festival of Sacrifice was extremely controversial among the missionaries. Some believed Christians should take a firm stand against the Festival of Sacrifice to let the community know the sacrifice is worthless and not pleasing to God. They refused to eat meat sacrificed at the Great Festival.

Because of this uncompromising belief that a Christian should never eat meat from the sacrifice, some Christians criticized me for accepting invitations to homes during the feast. Early in my missionary service I prayed over and struggled with the issue until I was satisfied that "He who eats meat, eats to the Lord, for he gives thanks to God; and he who abstains, does so to the Lord and gives thanks to God. . . . So then, each of us will give an account of himself to God" (Romans 14:6,12).

In retrospect, the effect on Moroccan believers, intelligent people with the same Holy Spirit to lead them in decisions as led us, was probably good. They had the opportunity to hear both viewpoints, and I'm sure our faithful Lord gave them a satisfying answer to use in their own quandary.

This settled, I was always happy to attend the celebration at the Festival of Sacrifice because meat was plentiful and people of limited means could entertain without embarrassment. I accepted the invitations whenever I could. In this setting, the story in Exodus 12 of the lamb slain and blood applied on the doorpost made a deep impression on my hearers. It also gave me another opportunity to share with friends about "the Lamb slain from the foundation of the world" (Revelation 13:8 NKJV).

Satanic Strongholds

Gaining an understanding of Islam and the religious customs woven so intricately into the fabric of Moroccan lives was only a small part of my "on-the-job training." Heathen customs – the power of saints, sorcery and charms – had a powerful hold on women in particular and generally brought gain to men. Moroccan women would pay a sorcerer everything they had in hopes of getting what they wanted. Sorcerers got wealthy in their profession, taking advantage of desperate and helpless women. Some sorcerers had several houses and wives.

In Souad's life we saw the extent of their belief in sorcery. Only one man had ever come to ask for her in marriage, and he did not have enough money to satisfy her mother. One day she told her parents she was coming to our house, but she never showed up. When I questioned her later, she confessed that she had gone to a sorcerer because she wanted to know why no one asked for her in marriage. The sorcerer promised he would take off the spell cast on her if she would bring more money. Eventually she married, no thanks to the sorcerer.

Another good friend of ours wanted her husband back after she had gotten a divorce. She sold the land he had given her in the divorce settlement and spent all her money on sorcery to get her husband back. Her efforts, however, were futile.

Charms consist of small pieces of paper with words from the Qur'an written on them. The papers are placed between pieces of felt or metal, usually brass. People tie charms on newborn babies, children and adults to ward off evil or illness, to heal or to bring a desired end.

Parents buy charms for their children and themselves. Sometimes they secretly place the charms where they hope the charms will work their power. Fatima was ironing in our home one day when I noticed a piece of paper attached to her hair. When I questioned her, she was shocked to find a charm she knew nothing about. She became agitated as she explained that she had spent the night before with her aunt. The family had wanted her to marry a cousin, but she refused. While she slept, they had slipped the charm into her hair. Although a believer, she took the charm seriously. I assured her she had nothing to fear, and we committed the matter to the Lord in prayer. He honored her desire, and she married a believer who loved her.

Throughout Morocco, the small, domed white buildings built over the graves of saints reminded me of the "high places" condemned by God in Scripture. In Meknes there is one called "the protector" of the city; another is titled "the healer." A long, winding path leads to this tomb, where the ill, the lame and the blind often gather. Women go to a saint's tomb to seek help for barrenness, to get back a husband who has strayed or to ask for help to obtain a divorce. They go to a saint's tomb as their last resort, when they have no power to change a situation. They take a rooster, goat, sheep or even a calf, some black olives, a loaf of bread. I often heard women bickering over which saint had the most power.

In the town of Khemisset lived a woman named Mimouna who paraded around town wearing a long, tattered dress tied at her waist with a rag. Her headdress, likewise ragged, was tied around her face for a veil, as was common to the area.

This woman knew a few English words, including some, learned from American servicemen, that I wouldn't want to repeat. Her favorite expression was "You crazy!" She tormented us constantly, leaning over the gate of our villa.

Children were terrified of her. One day I was on my way to a little boy's home to ask permission for him to go to camp. The boy was with me, showing me the way. I heard Mimouna yelling behind me, "This woman has come to lead small children astray and take them to hell!" The crowd was curious, and the little boy with me disappeared. I never saw him again.

After many similar incidents, I decided I had to discover more about Mimouna. Was she demon-possessed, simpleminded or mentally ill? Clem Payne, our spiritual mentor in many situations, read 1 John 4:1 to me: "Test the spirits to see whether they are from God." He suggested I talk to Mimouna about the blood of Christ or His death on the cross. If she opposed violently, I would know she was demon-possessed.

One day a rock crashed through my door, landing at my feet. Mimouna was leaning over the gate ready to revile me again. Much to her surprise, I invited her in for tea.

As we began to talk, I emphasized how God could not tolerate sin, nor could He dwell where sin existed. She denied that she had any sin, but agreed with me that God hated it. I emphasized the sin in her life, told her that Jesus died to save her from eternal punishment and stressed that His blood was the only remedy for sin. She responded that she had just seen Jesus the Sunday before down by the dam.

Once when a friend of ours was riding a horse, Mimouna came up behind him crying out, "You lost something!" He turned around to see what he might have dropped. "You lost your mind," she added with a laugh. I decided she was not simpleminded, but very clever.

Mimouna carried a stick with her as she walked around the village. One day she was caught coming out of a building with some missionaries' belongings. She dropped her stick and ran. I picked the stick up and took it home with me, placing it in a corner of the room. I don't know how she knew I had it, but every time she saw me she asked for her stick. And every time I refused.

One day when I got home the stick was gone. All the doors and windows were securely locked, and I saw her in the street with her stick! I never learned if Mimouna was demon–possessed, nor did my efforts to witness to her change her in any way.

Missionaries in North Africa soon learn the people fear demons. Moroccans may consider a doll that walks and talks or toys that move when wound as demon–possessed. They believe demons cause sickness, mental illness and drunkenness.

The Power of Evil Spirits

Demonism is alive and well in Morocco. It shows up in eerie ways when one is least expecting it. One day I was calling in the home of a girl whom I hoped to help spiritually. Another visitor was there, so I pondered over the Word of God, wondering what I could read that would not offend her. I chose the creation story and began to read.

The woman interrupted, crying out, "That is not the way the world was created. When the Prophet Muhammad was born, he brought the sun on his forehead and the moon on his back!" She began to dance around me, shouting loudly that I had come to deceive the people and lead them astray. I couldn't see any demons, but I surely felt them!

Wilma Harder Friesen, one of my fellow missionaries, had a similar experience at a home in Sefrou. A loud, threatening woman became agitated over a black headscarf Wilma wore. She demanded Wilma give it to her, which Wilma refused to do. The women in the home urged Wilma to give in to her. Fearful because the situation had gotten out of control, Wilma took a bowl of cold water and doused the woman, who immediately quieted down.

At a Berber funeral, missionary Evelyn Stenbock saw two women fall to the ground and thrash around on their hands and knees, grunting like pigs. Confusion reigned only for a moment. Some of the women's acquaintances quickly dug holes in the dirt floor beside the tent, poured water into them and thrust the women's faces into the muddy water. They snorted as if enjoying the mud puddle, creating a terrifying scene before coming out of the strange trance.

While these two women became "possessed" during funeral mourning, the sound of drums and music always drew two women who lived near Sunset Farm to dance. When they heard the music, they dropped whatever they were doing to hurry to the scene. There they would dance furiously for hours until they dropped. The husband of one of these women said, "If I bound her with chains she would break them and go. The demons call, and she must go."

Clearly, the multifaceted power we dealt with was far bigger than we were. But God had commissioned us to trust Him for wisdom, courage and protection, give out the gospel "to every creature" and leave the results to Him.

Chapter 7

The Dawn of an Exciting New Era

Following World War II, several U.S. military bases remained in Morocco. Five American servicemen stationed near Meknes often dropped by to visit us. Because the servicemen were far from home, they looked upon American missionaries as relatives. To them, a mission station was an English–speaking oasis with friendly inhabitants and good home cooking. American military personnel provided many benefits to the missionaries over the years, including food, material goods and much–appreciated volunteer labor.

During my first few weeks in Morocco, language study and getting acquainted with my new environment occupied most of my time. I had not gone outside the *medina* since the night I arrived. One day the soldiers took us to their base in a jeep. The countryside was beautiful – green fields splashed with wild red poppies, roses and other flowers; mountains; and parks.

What a contrast to the *medina*, with its dark, noisy streets, donkeys plodding under their heavy loads and hundreds of beggars and sleeping Arabs lining the narrow street. The beggars calling to us were almost more than I could bear. Because of wartime deprivation, the people still wore rags many of us wouldn't use for cleaning. They had no soap to launder them and no change of garments to wear while they did so. The fleas jumped onto our clothes as we passed.

Although our rare trips were wonderful, the *medina* was becoming my home, and my heart was there. I wouldn't have exchanged it for any place in the world. Whenever I returned from some excursion, I was always glad to get back home.

Learning to Communicate

I studied Arabic under the tutelage of experienced missionary Maude Cary. GMU's plan for language study included six months of intense grammar study followed by continued study. On our own we read an hour daily with a Moroccan tutor, who drilled us on pronunciation. We had an exam every three months over vocabulary and Bible stories.

Our maid was my main source for practicing conversation. She was superb – patient, giving me time to think through what I wanted to say and reading between the lines until we finally found a semblance of communication. And she was tolerant, overlooking many funny mistakes. The words for "mountain" and "garbage" sound alike at first. So do "heart" and "dog"! Imagine asking, "Will you take out the mountain?" Or telling the doctor you have a pain in your dog. Putting such mistakes into a religious context would bring disaster.

I had an awful time with some Arabic sounds. The tutor despaired when I couldn't say them correctly. The *kh* sound required a gentle scraping of the tonsils. *Ain* demanded a delicate tightening of the larynx – the opposite of when the doctor asks you to say "ahhh," which opens the throat. One day in despair the tutor ripped off his turban and, pointing to his bald head, cried out, "These scars are how I learned my Arabic lessons! I was beaten to help my memory!"

Luckily he didn't beat the lessons into my memory. I learned the difficult sounds as a child learns to talk, by listening and speaking, blurting it out, right or wrong.

I had been in Morocco only a week when Miss Cary sent me to the market alone. I knew a little French and so did the shopkeepers, so we managed. A month after my arrival, Miss Cary sent me to tell a family that a group of missionaries would soon arrive and to invite the family to a Sunday service. I nervously found my way through the narrow streets following Miss Cary's instructions, repeating the words I was to say. She knew where to send me for practice! The women of the home gave me a warm welcome and served tea.

I had learned John 3:16 in Arabic, and I thought it would be a good verse to use for my first witness in Morocco. I should have known better. I had been warned that the verse was controversial and that I shouldn't use it until I knew enough Arabic to explain the sonship of Jesus. We often learn the hard way, though. Once I had said my verse, my one–month vocabulary was about used up. My reward was being the butt of a joke. I was helpless to explain what the verse meant, and the women felt they knew a whole lot more than this young lady who couldn't even speak Arabic.

Fatima, the daughter of a woman who attended Miss Cary's women's class, often came to our home. I wanted to begin a girls' class, so I prepared a story and gave it first to Miss Cary for her approval and then to Fatima. Once Fatima understood what I said, I knew other girls would understand me, too. My level of understanding and fluency in Arabic increased almost daily.

One day, Miss Cary became ill, so she asked me to teach the women's class in her place. I used my flannelgraph material to help keep the women's attention, and I did well. My Arabic teacher was pleased with the results.

Before a year was up, I was calling the Friday women's class "our class." When Miss Cary's throat gave out, I could help with the singing and if necessary, I could take over and teach the class. It was done with great difficulty, but God's grace was sufficient. I knew that nothing but His grace could have helped me advance as quickly as I did. How good it is to give out the Word of God, no matter how feebly!

A Growing Mission Force

From where I sat in my little rooftop haven, I could look out over the walls of the city to the tower of the nearby mosque. From another window I could see the Jewish section, the *mellah*. Another direction gave me a view of the new city, the modern, beautiful European town. These views represented three different ethnic groups in need of the Savior. The more I became familiar with the land, the more I realized the extent of the spiritual darkness.

Religion was everywhere. I could never forget it because I had only to lift my eyes and look; if I didn't look, I heard the crier five times a day calling his people to pray. Hardly a sentence was spoken in any language without referring to

God. His name was on everyone's lips, but few had room for His Son in their hearts. It would be fair to say that most had never heard a clear presentation of the gospel. The harvest was apparent: it was laborers we needed.

Laborers were on the way! I was not alone as "the new missionary" for long. John and Alice Barcus, Moody Bible Institute graduates from Indiana, were right behind me, arriving in 1946, accompanied by a single woman, Sarah Peck. The Lord had called these three young people to witness to the Jews. We welcomed them with special delight, especially happy to have a man back on the team.

Bob and Doris Schneider along with Verna Janz were the next to come, traveling with Signe Johnson, who returned from furlough April 11, 1947. Before the year ended, missionaries filled every room of the house as God began to answer the prayer for ten men (along with a few good women). Life changed abruptly for us in August when the Schneiders' twin boys made a surprise entrance. Three weeks later, Joanna Barcus was born. It became a challenge to accomplish all the scheduling, preparation and work that go along with caring for three babies, housekeeping, language study, visitation and classes.

I bought a bicycle to help me get around in my ministry, but I didn't know how to ride it. The crowded streets were no place to learn, so I took it out to an open space, hoping to practice. Throngs gathered around to watch, so all I could do was stand there. Finally I discovered that by rising before daylight, I could reach the park as dawn was breaking. Riding up and down the garden paths with well–trimmed hedges on either side, I fell until bruises covered my body. By that time I had begun to draw an audience and had to return home. I was delighted when at last I could balance myself and not fall down.

I often biked out to the Berber village of Mijjot to teach the children. The people lived in tents, where the chickens meandered in to scratch or lay their eggs and the fleas felt at home. We sat under a fig tree for our classes, which allowed room for the neighbors, big and small, to gather around me. I told the story Miss Cary had approved, using the flannelgraph pictures as best I could and trying to make the gospel message clear. Even so, one old man, remembering the early missionary men, asked me to "preach."

How I loved the ragged little children, especially the little girls. Their society considered them "donkeys" and thought they couldn't learn. I knew that was not true. I prayed for the day there would be schools in the villages, schools even the little girls could attend. I envisioned these children evangelizing their own people and great changes occurring in the country villages.

For Christmas 1948, a group of us hired a carriage and went to the village to carry the story of Jesus to the Berbers. We sang a few songs and choruses in Arabic, and I presented the Christmas story with flannelgraph. Then we distributed oranges, Christmas card pictures, little kimonos for the babies and toddlers and ribbons for the older children to tie around their heads. They were thrilled with these gifts.

Fortunately, Miss Cary, our senior missionary and language teacher, loved the young missionaries and put up with all our antics, mistakes and enthusiasm. She was delighted with the babies. Joanna Barcus' parents moved to Sefrou, but the twins remained at Derb Skat. Danny Schneider became her special charge, while I was David's nanny. Doris Schneider had served as the breakfast cook until the twins were born; then Bob took over that job. With our help, Doris got through Arabic language study and took part in the ministry.

She and I worked like sisters in child evangelism, setting up the flannelgraph and sharing the ministry in many ways. Vance Payne, three years old when his parents arrived in Morocco, was the only child in my English Sunday school, but I held a class for him anyway.

During the most crowded year in Derb Skat, "Grandma" Cary slept in an upstairs room divided into two small rooms. Two single missionary women, Verna Janz and Beulah Weston, shared the other side of that room. The Schneiders and Clem and Dorothea Payne, with their little son Vance, took the rooms on the lower floor. The Barcuses had the large bedroom on the second floor. I, of course, slept in my haven on the roof. One side of the divided living room became a tiny guest room that housed many distinguished guests. Don P. Shidler, vice president of GMU, spent a month in Morocco in April 1947 to get acquainted with the field. To provide guidance and mentoring to the young men, GMU President G. Christian Weiss spent several months on the field.

A long table stretched across the dining room to hold the large group. It took ages for everyone to get to the table and be served, and just as long for them to depart. The social aspect of communal living was hard on language study. It caused me, especially, to squirm with impatience.

Miss Cary wrote in the annual report that "1947 was the best year our Morocco Mission has passed in a long time." In Meknes new missionaries had arrived, with more on the way to fill the language school; new women were attending the weekly classes; and classes for boys and girls were growing.

We opened a small book shop, "The Lighthouse," where the men spent late afternoons selling scripture portions. Mehdi Ksara, a believer who preached and sang, prepared gospel recordings in Arabic that were played over a loudspeaker. Jelali, the young man who was baptized in 1947, also had a good voice and was a fine speaker. Bob Schneider made recordings of messages Miss Cary wrote out for Jelali to read. Bob also recorded several messages by G. Christian Weiss while he was visiting. And Joy Ridderhoff had begun her Gospel Recordings ministry, giving us a few other records in Moroccan Arabic, which we played as well.

Our group was outgrowing Derb Skat. With Signe Johnson's return from her furlough, it was time for the new missionaries to begin to spread out. Miss Johnson went to Sefrou to reopen the station there. She took Sarah Peck with her to Sefrou, where they reclaimed a small rented house on the city wall.

Chapter 8

The Work Branches Out

As early as 1905, missionaries used the mountain town of Sefrou as a base to contact Berbers. Sefrou, an old inland town south of Fes, a European "new city" for French officials, had a large Jewish population and the usual Arab and Berber townspeople. Signe Johnson was in charge of the station during World War II, but a shortage of personnel led to its close at the end of the war. Missionaries remained at the Meknes station while Signe and Maude Cary went on furlough.

Sefrou had close to 18,000 townspeople, quite evenly divided between Arabs and Jews. Every major center had a special market day each week. Sefrou's was Thursday. Throngs of country people crowded the streets that day to sell produce and buy necessities.

Many of them were well acquainted with missionaries, some from childhood, when Enyart, Swanson and Reed had lived for long periods in village homes. Victor Swanson once had a shop in Sefrou where he made many Jewish friends. Both Jewish and Muslim children had heard the gospel through the classes Miss Cary – whom they called "Miss Terri" – had held in her younger years. Because of their contact with her, the townspeople called all the missionaries, even Signe Johnson, "Miss Terri," both as a curse and as a loving name. Many of these children grew up to be shopkeepers, and some became officials in the town.

The mission owned land just outside one of Sefrou's gates. For years officials had denied the mission a building permit, but the climate now changed. The time had come to build. Supervising the operation fell to John Barcus, who was still studying French and Arabic and commuting from Meknes. Building supplies, most transported from Fes and Casablanca, were costly and hard to obtain, sometimes available only on the black market. The mission bought a two–ton, French–built truck to save money by hauling their own supplies – not an easy task because of gas rationing. John found the builders less than enthusiastic over their work.

It was a relief to John and Miss Johnson to have GMU's president come, not to observe, but to sweat with them on this huge building project. G. Christian Weiss was fluent in the language, knowledgeable about the country and customs and gifted in dealing with people. With his help, such things as obtaining rations of cement and iron for the building fell into place.

The Sefrou property was lower on one side than on the other, so they dug a basement and built three rooms and a garage under half the house. Ground level at the front door, the upper story had ten rooms and a meeting hall for classes and preaching services. The plan was to get enough of the house ready for occupancy so the women could move into it. That would allow the Barcus family to move to a rented house until their own apartment was ready. Eventually the building would become a language study center.

I never lived in Sefrou, but it was an exciting place to visit. People of all ages dropped in unannounced for a cup of coffee, a piece of bread and a dose of God's Word. I spent one of my first vacations in Sefrou. It was a rare treat to sit in on Miss Johnson's classes and listen to the remarks these young men made concerning the gospel. When Miss Johnson suggested the possibility of a church in Sefrou, one young man sadly shook his head and said it could never be because of the Muslims.

There were many converts in Sefrou over the years – men, women and children who stood true to Christ against great odds. Many people, though, called the mission house "the House of the Blasphemers." More than once the mayor placed a guard in the street to keep people from coming in. Those attending meetings were beaten or hindered in other ways, and more than once Miss Johnson wiped spit off her cheeks.

The Barcuses and other missionaries had fruitful experiences in Sefrou. Among them was the discipling of young Jews who eventually left Morocco in a great exodus to Israel. Thirty years later, after his wife, Alice, had died, John Barcus made two trips to Israel. In miraculous ways, he located five Sefrou converts who had emigrated to Israel. Most still stood true in their faith. One of them, overwhelmed by the visit, cried, "For twenty years I dreamed that you would one day come to visit me here in Israel; then I stopped dreaming – but here you are!"

The Base for Ministry

Back at Derb Skat, things kept on humming. A whole roster of new missionaries passed through, including some bound for GMU's work in the Sudan, stopping in Morocco for French study. Later, some of our missionaries en route to France and Switzerland stopped in Meknes for a year of French study.

Miss Cary was praying for the day when a new station could be opened at El Hajeb, a town she knew from the early days. Young men from there had visited Derb Skat and listened intently to the gospel. They invited us to open a station in their town.

Picture Meknes as the pivotal point on a compass: Tangier is about 200 miles north; Fes is about an hour's drive east; Sefrou is nestled in the mountains a half hour south of Fes. Khemisset is an hour's drive west, on the road to the capital city of Rabat and its sister city, Sale. Beyond Rabat is Casablanca.

The first town south of Meknes, El Hajeb, is about thirty miles across the plains. El Hajeb is a small Berber town built on the cliffs below the evergreen forests and snow-capped peaks. Under French rule the area became a summer resort playground, with winter ski facilities. As you approach the town by highway, a great, eyebrow-shaped mass of rock rises before you: *el hajeb*, the eyebrow.

Typically, there was resistance to renting a house to us "infidels." Finally, however, a small one was found. Reluctantly we helped Miss Cary move out of Derb Skat. She was leaving a significant work in the hands of enthusiastic, dedicated novices, letting go so the new generation could take over. At seventy years of age, Miss Cary was ready to take on a new challenge. She was also involved in final work on a new Arabic hymnal (which she wrote out by hand) and Bible lessons for us to use. Later the mission purchased a house in El Hajeb.

George Weiss helped locate another home in Meknes for some personnel. It was called *derb taum*, "the alley of food," in reference to couscous, the common pasta meal of Morocco. Derb Taum was in a poor section of Meknes not far from the *mellah*, making it a wonderful location for Jewish children's classes. Clem and Dorothea Payne moved there, allowing Clem to make necessary repairs on the house. When it was time for them to move on, they settled in Khemisset.

Khemisset was just a small town when our mission bought the first property there before World War II. The French had built a hospital, post office, bus station, French school, police station and a few government buildings.

To encourage European immigration, the government offered free land to anyone who would build a home on it. Because of this, the town had a small European population living in comfortable villas. Most of the other homes in the town were *nualas*, round mud huts with grass thatch roofs or more progressive oblong rooms with corrugated tin roofs.

Our first house there was in the French neighborhood, a villa with a big, walled-in yard. We saw Khemisset develop into a city, with properly laid-out streets and numbers on the houses. *Nualas* became a relic of the past, replaced by building codes because of the fire hazard.

When I got to Morocco, the Khemisset station was busy with girls' classes and with girls who lived in the home of Ellen Doran and Emmagene Coats. One new missionary, Elsie Regier, was a tall, outgoing Kansan, gifted in the language and capable of almost any task handed to her. She began her language study in Khemisset with Ellen as her grammar teacher. Elsie's fiance, Peter Z. Friesen, came to Morocco about two years later. We had the joy of holding a missionary wedding in Derb Skat.

The Schools Begin

As usual, the Lord had things timed perfectly. From the time I arrived in Morocco, Miss Cary had talked about the need for a Bible institute for young men. She believed the future evangelization of Morocco would depend upon well-prepared Moroccan evangelists. The subject arose frequently as the mission staff grew. Finally, in January 1951, the Field Council met and appointed a committee to take steps toward the formation of a Bible institute. The plans were to include both material and spiritual preparation.

The committee chose a location: Sunset Farm. British missionary Charles Fraser–Smith had placed Sunset Farm in the hands of a Moroccan manager when he left Morocco before World War II. His wife's illness and subsequent death made his return impossible, so Fraser–Smith prayed for the right party to buy the farm two and a half miles from Khemisset. He contacted two mission organizations, but each turned his offer down. Remembering Victor and Nellie Swanson's hospitality and friendship when he had first arrived in Khemisset, he decided to contact GMU.

Fraser–Smith notified his attorney in Morocco to arrange for the sale he had negotiated with GMU at a ridiculously low price. It included some land the mission could sell to pay for the property. The attorney was stunned. He immediately called Fraser–Smith in England to say that he could not allow the sale of the property at that price. The two men argued over the proposed sale, but Fraser–Smith had made up his mind. The attorney appealed and refused to act unless Fraser–Smith raised the price.

The matter was not debatable for Fraser–Smith. God's work had been done on that farm, and he was selling it to people who would continue to do God's work. Finally the attorney gave in. "I will continue with the sale, Monsieur

Fraser–Smith." He was confident, however, that Fraser–Smith was bankrupting himself.

God honored Fraser–Smith's commitment. In 1948 the final papers were signed for the transfer of Sunset Farm to Gospel Missionary Union. A Spanish Christian couple occupied the house with Elsie Regier. After Pete and Elsie were married on January 27, 1949, they began their life together on the farm.

Plans for the Men's Bible School moved right along. Bob and Doris Schneider were chosen to head the school. Pete and Elsie left to open the final GMU station in the city of Sale, an ancient coastal town across the river from the capital city of Rabat. Pete became one of Morocco's finest colporteurs, traveling from place to place selling Scriptures and preaching. He eventually returned to manage Sunset Farm.

The Men's Bible School at Sunset Farm was operating successfully, and we realized that the time had come to train women for Christian service as well. A couple from Tangier expressed their desire to send two girls to me to learn to read and to receive Bible training. Two girls from Meknes and one from Khemisset also asked to come.

Early in 1954 we began looking for a suitable house in which to begin a Girls' Bible School. Fraser–Smith's house in Khemisset, next door to the mission property and occupied by a pharmacy, became available. The mission bought this house, so conveniently located and already divided into two apartments. Elsie Friesen, Doris Schneider and I started making Moroccan–style beds and mattresses and getting the property ready for occupancy.

One month after purchasing the house, we started school with three girls as charter students. About twenty–five women and girls attended the opening–day services on October 4, 1954. An outstanding Bible woman from Rabat challenged the girls to seize the opportunity before them. Other missionaries and Moroccan Christians spoke at the three services that day.

Our group of missionaries came from many different backgrounds with varied educational advantages, but we were all high school graduates with at least Bible institute training under our belts. We had decided to hold six-week terms for the Khemisset Girls' School. In this third-world country where girls rarely received an education, we couldn't parallel their training with our own. We planned a curriculum suited to their needs.

Mornings were spent in Bible study and literacy classes. In the afternoons, we taught sewing and knitting and sold the finished products to help pay for the students' expenses during the term. Before long, the students were teaching a weekly girls' class at the school while local women met for a Bible study taught by missionaries in another room.

In the three years the Men's Bible School was in existence, three men graduated. Although we had several terms of the girls' school, no one ever graduated. Only eternity will show the value of this work, not the least of which was the maturing of the missionaries, our growing faith in God's ability and our deepened understanding of the Word as we readied ourselves for the ministry of teaching.

Chapter 9

The Battle for Souls Begins

When I arrived in Morocco in 1946, Americans were highly respected because of their role in reclaiming North Africa after World War II. The country was under the protection of the French government, giving missionaries considerable freedom. In the 1912 treaty making Morocco a French protectorate, France had promised not to bring pork into the country or to propagate Christianity. The agreement placed no restrictions on European worship. The steeples of great French cathedrals and Protestant churches attested to this fact, adding character and beauty to the skylines of Casablanca and other seaports. Realistically, though, the agreement allowed no proselytizing among Muslims.

But what Frenchman can live without pork? The French didn't keep their agreement about pork, nor were they concerned about the proselytizing clause. Under French rule, we registered as evangelical missionaries and went about our witness openly, all the while enjoying favor with the government.

The Moroccan king responsible for negotiating the 1912 treaty had had personal reasons for doing so. He had in effect called in a European police force to subdue his warring tribes. It was a "peace–at–any–price" measure to keep his own dynasty on the throne.

As for France's benefit from the treaty, she obtained a vast new region of fertile land with an ideal climate in which to expand her agricultural interests. During the protectorate years, the French found the Berbers – whom the Arabs had failed to subdue – to be willing, cheap and competent farm labor. The Berbers quickly learned European farming methods and obtained new skills, new crops, new equipment and a new language.

South of the Atlas Mountains, arid Sahara land became a valley of roses, commercially grown for Parisian perfumes.

Central Morocco was ideal for growing jasmine and other rare fragrances. Along the coast the French obtained the natural cork forest that runs across Morocco and up into Spain. This provided an endless supply of corks for the wineries that processed truckloads of grapes from the acres of vineyards the French planted. Citrus fruit, melons, plums, cherries, apricots and every vegetable imaginable filled the orchards, trucks, gardens and markets of Morocco.

France changed Morocco from a Barbary Coast nation to a modern civilization. The French built highways, railroads, hospitals, schools, libraries and orphanages, established law and order and created a government bureaucracy unsurpassed in the skill of producing red tape.

When the Arabs conquered North Africa in the seventh century, they had won an empty victory. They had gained converts to Islam, but not loyal subjects. The Berbers remained hostile and treacherous, a law unto themselves. The Arabs found it impossible to bring them under control. France, on the other hand, subdued the tribes by cultivating their skills and educating their children, and for several decades peace prevailed.

Revolution

As time went on, Berbers moved into supervisory, industrial and government jobs. When I arrived in 1946, I heard many marketplace speeches by Arabs protesting what they saw as favoritism. I became used to living in the midst of conflict – conflict that grew steadily worse.

One day in 1949, some of our missionaries went to Casablanca to pick up some girls for camp. They learned that an uprising had occurred the day before. To reach the girls, the missionaries had to crawl under broken wires and rubble. Frenchmen had been beheaded in the street in front of the girls, who had many horrible stories to tell when they got to camp.

Morocco had moved into a state of revolution. From then on, European civilians became the target of unprovoked surprise attacks. The nationalistic spirit grew rapidly to alarming proportions. The Sultan of Morocco tried to oust the French government and all other foreign influences, including us. Blood ran freely.

Just when we thought the nationalistic movement had gained control of Morocco, news came of the sudden dethroning of the Sultan. In a desperate move in 1953 to stop the terrorism, the French banished him from the country – first to Corsica and then to distant Madagascar. The country went into mourning, donning black garments, and the terrorism increased.

The Ministry Grows

I spent my first four years in Morocco at Derb Skat. As the other missionaries moved to different locations, I settled down with the Schneider family to carry on the many responsibilities of that big house. David and Danny, the twin Schneider boys, became my special charges. I often stayed with them while their mother and father went to visit markets and preach to the people.

When the twins were three years old, I spent a month away from the family. After that, every time I left the house on an errand they cried at the door until I returned, afraid I had left them again. Their sister, Sue, was also born at Derb Skat during that first term, so I had another doll to play with. What a blessing it was to have a "family" when I was so far away from my own loved ones.

We were a growing family, with new missionaries coming to join us and little ones being born. There was a large, extended family of lively "aunts," "uncles" and "cousins" all over Morocco. When speaking to any of us, Moroccans referred to the male missionaries as "your brothers" and to the women as "your sisters." Some thought we truly were related, so our explanation of the fellowship and love that bound us together was a testimony to the unity we had in Christ.

Derb Taum, El Hajeb and Sefrou were, like Derb Skat, "Grand Central" stations – there was always someone at the door, always homes to visit, always classes to prepare. Two and later three households buzzed in Khemisset. The Friesens built a *nuala* – the large, round, native–style hut with a thatched roof – for services at the farm. They also began a first–aid ministry to neighboring tent people at the entrance to the farm. As plans for the Men's Bible School progressed, the missionaries remodeled a stable into a kitchen, dormitory and classrooms. Expansion kept a full–time building program going there.

I traveled from one station to another each summer to conduct Vacation Bible Schools. With the help of two other women, we began a girls' camp at Sunset Farm, where we also held boys' camps every summer. We reinstated nationwide Bible conferences for Moroccan believers and an annual missionary prayer conference.

Sale and later Rabat were busy stations. We taught, preached, built, planned and pressed forward in the work of the Lord. Every advance was a victory as we reclaimed territory once served by the pioneers and moved into new and exciting ministries. The Lord answered our prayer for ten men on the field – in 1954 we took a photo of the ten men at the missionary conference.

These enthusiastic and talented young men and their wives pushed forward in colportage work, teaching in the Men's Bible School, witnessing in markets, preparing for widespread literature ministry and operating camps and conferences. There were baptisms and the first marriage of two Christian Arabs, and we witnessed the return of scattered believers who began coming back to services. We wrote in the 1954 annual report, "Morocco for Christ is our goal!"

Health Problems

Small wonder, then, that Satan began to plague us in earnest. Even as the revolution was nipping at our heels, we began to experience discouraging illnesses and major catastrophes. Maude Cary developed pemphigus, a dreadful blistering skin disease. Finally, in great distress and with no help for her misery, she was flown to the United States, courtesy of the U.S. Air Force.

Miss Cary recovered and returned to her beloved Morocco, but David Hazen did not. He was flown home in an iron lung, a victim of polio. He later recovered but could not return to Morocco. Dave and two other new men, Don Peterson and Bob Peabody, had served in Morocco during World War II and returned as missionaries. A kerosene heater exploded in the El Hajeb house, burning Don Peterson badly.

Because Maude Cary was elderly and had been sick, we began to consider the need for a burial ground. John Barcus began arranging for permission to set aside a cemetery on Sunset Farm. Miss Cary served to retirement and was buried years later in Kansas City. Reluctantly, we met at the little lot for the first time when John and Alice Barcus buried their baby, Jimmy.

Strong, exuberant, talented Elsie Regier Friesen, who had helped so much at the Girls' School we operated together, went into a coma at the supper table one evening. An English-trained midwife and the doctor came. They decided to rush her to the capital city, Rabat. John Barcus met them outside the city to guide them to the hospital and interpret for them. It was toxemia.

Both Elsie and the baby she was carrying died that terrifying night, leaving Pete, his three little children and the missionary family in shock. A few years later Virgil, Elsie's youngest son, died of leukemia at six years of age and was buried in the same cemetery.

Illness and death in the missionary family were heavy trials, but there were other battles as well. Besides the revolution, terrorist attacks, sickness and catastrophes, a religious cult preyed on converts and dogged inquirers at every mission station. Our only recourse was prayer. In time, the Lord took care of the situation when the cult departed from the area.

Protection Amid Unrest

That summer I went to Meknes for Vacation Bible School – always a big event. Three local Christian girls helped us. Some days as many as fifty girls came, displaying an unusual spirit of quietness, reverence and obedience. Several girls professed salvation and others gave public testimony for the first time. We invited the mothers to the closing day exercises. Nearly seventy-five people crowded into the Derb Skat court.

Later in the summer, three of the Christian girls were baptized. Until then, all of the relatives of the candidates for baptism had either opposed or showed no interest in attending the services. Now, for the first time, two mothers attended.

Throughout the revolution we lost neither buildings nor lives, though the vegetation on Sunset Farm was set on fire several times. All the occupants of the farm worked night and day to extinguish the grass fires.

The Lord used the ministry of the first-aid station and our good relationship with the surrounding tribes to spare our lives and property. Along the road beyond our farm and throughout Morocco, foreign-owned farms were devastated. Colonists who escaped with only the clothes on their backs were the fortunate ones; many others were killed and their farms burned.

Missionaries caught in the midst of foreign revolutions have two options: go or stay. With so many ministries in progress, leaving the country was unthinkable. We stayed and adjusted to the uneasy atmosphere as did the Moroccans, who could not leave.

Unrest could break out anywhere. Once, while at the bus station in Meknes, we watched a truckload of French soldiers pass the station and drive into an open space in front of the market, where a crowd of protesters had gathered. The soldiers opened fire upon the masses of young people, many of whom died.

We sensed the growing political unrest, but we put our lives in God's hands and kept on working.

Chapter 10

Trusting Through Turmoil:
The Revolution Years

Picture yourself in a Moroccan home, seated on a plush couch in the living room. Family members have gathered for a meal, some seated on the floor, others on couches beside you. You have just finished sipping a leisurely glass of sweet mint tea when a low round table is brought in. A *ta-jeen* is set before you – a succulent meat stew browned in oil and spices, simmered to perfection and served with all its juices in a round, flat dish. It may be topped with plump raisins, prunes, olives, almonds, quince or whatever vegetables are in season.

The host picks up a flat, round loaf of fresh–baked bread, breaks it and hands a piece to each person. "*Bismillah!* (Partake in the name of God!)" he or she murmurs and leads the way by breaking off a bite-sized piece of bread to dip in the meat juice. Without hesitation, everyone dips in and begins to eat heartily. Meanwhile, the host urges on, "*Kool, kool!* Eat, eat! Don't be ashamed; make yourself at home, just eat!"

On Throne Day, October 26, 1956, I was enjoying such a meal in the home of an English–trained nurse in Khemisset. The holiday commemorated a long–awaited announcement one year earlier that the 1912 Treaty of Fes making Morocco a protectorate of France had ended. The beloved exiled king would be coming back home. In the twelve months that followed, the promises had come true as the country elbowed its way to independence.

In the company of good friends, the mood around the table was festive. We had just begun to dip our bread into the *ta-jeen* when a young man burst into the front room and yelled to the nurse, "A bomb just went off in a crowd! They're bringing the injured to the hospital! Hurry! Hurry! They need your help!"

The nurse jumped up and, leaving her dinner, ran to the hospital two blocks away. The scene was chaotic and shocking. She came first to a friend, Ahmed, who was near death. He had been changing a light bulb when the bomb exploded under him. "Help me," he cried weakly. She knelt down and tried to stop the blood spurting from his wounds, but it was too late. He did not survive.

She moved on to Abd el Kader, a lad who came regularly to my classes for boys. He lived, but he lost a leg. Some died that night and many were wounded.

The Sultan Returns

Earlier in 1956, after much bloodshed and tragedy, the French had turned the country back over to its Arab rulers. Excitement had bordered on hysteria. Moroccans claimed to see the exiled Sultan in the moon each evening several weeks before his return. Crowds of people gathered on the roofs to see this amazing phenomenon. I went up with them and gazed at the moon until my eyes grew bleary, but I didn't have enough faith or imagination to see him.

Stories spread that the Sultan's airplane had flown in from Paris without any gas, landing safely in Rabat, the capital of Morocco. Many believed this, and even today these stories are passed on to new generations.

At the scheduled moment a huge DC–6B appeared over Rabat, accompanied by a dozen fighter planes and followed by a Constellation G. This was it: the long–awaited, dreamed–of return from exile of Sidi Muhammad Ben Youssef, Sultan of Morocco! The pent–up excitement and expectation of a whole nation exploded into one grand "*Yahiya El Malik*! Long live the king!" as the wheels of his plane touched the soil of his native country. It had been more than two years since he had been whisked off to involuntary exile.

As the Sultan and his two recognized sons, the princes, stepped from the first plane, the crowd cheered and greeted them. The princesses, wives and other family members slipped quietly from the second plane into their waiting vehicles. After the proper exchange of greetings, the royal convoy began its triumphal procession along the seven-mile trip from the airport to the palace.

First came the trucks, mounted with loudspeakers exhorting the thousands of faithful subjects along the road to calm and order. Next was the *pasha* (the lord-mayor) of Rabat, who, at the official entry of the city, made the traditional offering of milk and dates to his majesty.

The princesses followed, then the four members of the regency council and other dignitaries. There were the usual motorcycle escort and the Sultan's own Black Guard in brilliant scarlet and white, mounted on magnificent horses.

It took a full forty minutes to cover the flag-bedecked course. At the edge of the city, a gigantic triumphal arch of scaffolding entirely covered with palm fronds spanned the road.

Some 15,000 guards kept remarkable order, but now and then a humble subject would break through the ranks and dash up to kiss his sovereign's hand. One hundred thousand people pressed forward in undulating waves to catch a closer glimpse of their monarch as he passed through the principal gate to his imperial residence.

The Moroccans continued their rejoicing for several days and nights, celebrating their king's return and his declaration of independence from foreign domination. Trucks and taxis carrying chanting human cargo traveled from all over Morocco for the occasion. They wove through the streets not blocked off by singers and dancers.

Why not celebrate? The king had come home! The simple Moroccan flag, a green star in a solid red field, waved over a sovereign independent state that aspired to a recognized place among other nations.

Among the missionaries, however, many questions arose about the future. This was a momentous chapter in the country's history. Morocco would never be the same again.

Would independence harm the missionary work in Morocco? More important still, what would the future return of our true King be like? How many Moroccans would be ready to welcome Him?

Violence Increases

After Morocco gained her independence on March 2, 1956, a new flood of religious fervor swept over the country. The Sultan deplored the continuing acts of violence and terrorism. The first Friday after he returned from France with the signed Declaration of Independence, he prayed and spoke to a large crowd in the historic old ruins of the Mosque of Hassan in Rabat, the capital city. He praised "the virtues that have made Islam great: justice, tolerance, sense of duty, respect for the human person," and he exhorted Muslims to remain faithful to the traditions and principles of Islam.

The king, a moderate, meant to implore tolerance toward Christians and Jews, but his fanatical subjects focused on "the traditions and principles of Islam" as a mandate to persecute Christians and Jews.

The Throne Day riot in Khemisset was only one of many following the king's return. Just a short time before, rioting had broken out in Meknes, with many Europeans massacred and many more injured. Almost 400 European farms around the Meknes region were burned. As I visited homes in El Hajeb that day, I wondered why I was receiving cold receptions, unaware that a demonstration against foreigners was going on in Meknes. A sniper had shot and killed the leader of the party that had led the fight for independence. Rumor said a Frenchman had murdered him. The whole city was in an uproar.

When I learned about the riot, I ran to tell the El Hajeb missionaries about it. Late that night we heard a popping noise that sounded like gunshots. We thought an army on the hill was attacking the European army, but that was not true. In the morning we discovered that the lumberyard had been set on fire. The "gunshots" had been roof tiles that crackled as they broke and burned. We looked down upon the beautiful valley between El Hajeb and Meknes where hundreds of French farm homes still burned.

Bob and Doris Schneider had started toward Meknes that day to shop. When stones began to roll across the road in front of their car, they turned around and went back to Khemisset.

After they left, every car on that road was stopped, the occupants dragged out and killed. A pottery kiln was set on fire, and when the occupants tried to escape, they were pushed into the flames to die.

A Spanish believer in Meknes left his place of work to hurry home to his wife. He was caught but released, while others behind him met a terrible fate. Daniel could not explain how he had been spared, except that God had intervened.

Telephones were cut off in El Hajeb. Newspapers were not available. We had to depend on friends to keep us informed about what they heard. We were concerned about our co-workers in Meknes and elsewhere.

After several days, since everything seemed calm, I took my customary trip to Khemisset, which required traveling by taxi to the city of Meknes. I walked out to the place the taxis loaded and got my ride. Only Arab and Berber men were traveling.

The conversation in the taxi quickly focused on the riot. One man said, "A Frenchman started this bloodshed, otherwise it would not have happened. Now if this foreign woman doesn't start a riot, we will have no trouble." He had no idea I could understand him, so I shocked him when I retorted, "Relax! I don't plan to start a riot!"

As the taxi passed one farm, the men explained that every member of the household had been killed. When the policemen came for the bodies, they too were murdered.

Instead of letting me off at the bus station in the European section of Meknes, the driver drove directly to the old *medina*. I grabbed my bag and walked to Derb Skat, expecting Verna Janz and Mildred Swan to take me in. A kindly Arab man accompanied me, concerned for my safety. When we reached Derb Skat, I pounded on the door, but there was no answer.

I took the city bus to the bus station in the new part of town. We passed stores with plate-glass windows broken out. The streets were smeared with blood. Rioters had used broken glass to slash the throats of their helpless victims.

I boarded a bus and finally arrived safely in Khemisset. How relieved my co-workers were to see me! "Where are Verna and Swannee?" they asked. I told them about my trip through Meknes and said I had no idea where our colleagues were.

Later we received a telegram from our co-workers, sent from the city of Fes. They had been on their way home from Tangier by train when the riot started. Because of the riot, the train did not stop in Meknes.

God protected the missionaries, and order was finally restored around Meknes. Bitter hatred toward all foreigners, however, could be felt for a long time.

A Lesson on Sacrifice

Near the end of 1956, Morocco was admitted as a member of the United Nations. As she settled into her new role as an independent nation, the frightening years of massacres and rioting finally ended.

Bob Schneider had started an annual Fall Prayer Conference and invited missionaries from all five societies working in the country. We met at a lake resort a few miles inland from Khemisset for the first two conferences. In 1953 we held the first fall conference at Sunset Farm.

Throughout the year, Bob collected and published prayer requests, which he circulated to the missionaries twice a year. The turbulent years of revolution drew all the missionaries closer as we shared the joys and sorrows common to all of us.

We met for the prayer conference in September 1956, acknowledging that we didn't know all the answers concerning living and witnessing for Christ in this turbulent land. Together we praised the Lord for His protection and for the victories He had given us. Every advance we could make would be on our knees, one day at a time. While we couldn't foresee what God had planned, many of us believed He was preparing us for greater work. We began to investigate our methods and adapt them to the challenge of a new day.

A while after the revolution, two young fellows came to visit me in my home in Khemisset. I noticed one had a hand missing. When I asked about it, he explained that during the revolution he had picked up a bomb that exploded in his hand.

"But I would be willing to give not only my hand but my whole life for my country!" he added emphatically.

This bold statement bothered me then and still does today. How many of us would be willing to give a hand or our life – or even a little bit of comfort – to reach a lost world for Christ?

Chapter 11

Berbers of the Barbary Coast

Before I move on, I want to keep my promise to tell you more about my experiences with the Berbers near Meknes and about the origin and customs of the Berber race.

People who know me well might think of my ministry as primarily oriented to city–dwellers. That was so, since the demands on my time increased with all our added activities, allowing me less time to spend in rural ministry.

Yet even in the city we ministered to Berbers. Meknes, Khemisset, Sefrou and El Hajeb were all ancient Berber marketing centers. Arab conquerors settled in them, the French modernized them and the cities grew.

At all of our stations, many Berbers we worked with spoke Arabic. We rarely needed to use Shilha, their mother tongue, unless we visited communities away from town. Arabic and French were our primary languages in city ministry.

The revolution removed all but the most stalwart Europeans – only a few of the brave and dedicated stayed on to continue medical and educational vocations. Most of the Jews left, too. We had front–row seats to watch prophecy be fulfilled as excited Jewish professional people, craftsmen and government workers joined a voluntary exodus to Israel.

Like Pharaoh of old, Morocco was reluctant to let these key citizens go. Many Jewish families slipped out secretly at night to waiting ships or obtained temporary permission to travel, never to return. Suddenly there was a huge vacuum of job openings available to the few Moroccans educated by the French – and an urgent need to educate all Muslim children, rich or poor.

Following independence, Berbers flooded into the towns. The populations of all our target cities exploded. The years brought amazing changes. Most important, the public–school system opened its doors to all boys and girls, blending Berbers and Arabs into a sophisticated population – profoundly independent, multilingual and world-conscious.

Our Berber mission field had come to our doorstep. We hoped to win and train Berbers to take the gospel back to their own people, and our ministry concentrated to a large extent on doing that.

The Berber People

Living with Maude Cary my first years in Morocco was rewarding in many ways. Not the least of these rewards were her tales of her first years in Morocco. Single and in her twenties, she had been engaged for a time to George Reed, one of four men who spent long periods living with various Berbers. Maude had even learned Shilha.

Maude Cary was living in Fes when a fanatic who had come to town to kill a Christian shot an English missionary of North Africa Mission. It was 1903, and the Boxer massacres in China were fresh in the minds of GMU missionaries, so they left for the coast. They later chided themselves about that flight – they should have trusted God to keep them safe. Eventually they returned to Fes and finally to Meknes, vowing never to run away from blessing again.

Miss Cary also recounted experiences the missionary men had while living with the Berbers. In 1905, Frank Enyart lived in a mountain Berber town with huge houses made of earthen bricks. Such castles often contained a dozen families. Although a clan would unite solidly to resist an attack by another clan, feuds would split it and members of the clan would shoot at one another from the roofs of their castle houses.

One day while Enyart took a bath at a spring, he laid aside some of his clothes, with his watch in a pocket. Two boys, sons of his host, watched Enyart bathe and soon disappeared. When Enyart put his clothes back on, he noticed his watch was missing. He went to the house and related the incident to his host. A grim look came over the man's face.

He took his rifle down from the wall, said, "Come with me," and went over to where his son was sitting with a group of friends. He cocked his rifle, looked sternly at his son and said, "If you don't tell me where the foreigner's watch is, I'll put this bullet through you." The boy turned pale and produced the watch.

Such friends as Enyart's host took the missionaries into their homes under the custom called *mizrug-allah*, a vow of personal protection in the name of God. Without a *mizrug* to protect him, no foreigner could ever have hoped to pass through, let alone stay in, a Berber community safely.

Other customs that make up the law for Berbers are the unity of the clan, tribal honor, the vendetta (or blood revenge), the refuge (by which a man can escape punishment if he reaches the home of a man who will take him in), the *dabeeha* (sacrifice of a sheep or ox in the presence of one from whom some request is to be made – a request that he can't refuse), and the *halfa* (oath) of a witness to swear to an accused person's innocence. Laws of the land may mean little to a Berber, but he trembles to break any of these traditional laws of his own people. The *mizrug-allah* agreement was probably in the mind of the father in the above situation.

While the mountain people built castles, the plains people lived in woven tents combining the fiber of the palmetto plant with goat hair and wool. Women gather the plants and spin and weave the heavy material into strips. The men sew the strips together and raise the tent. As a tent ages, a new strip is added each year to keep it in good repair. The strips are boiled in pomegranate peelings to preserve them from the weather. Since pomegranate peelings are a natural black dye, Moroccan Berber tents are black. In hot weather, Berbers roll up the sides of their tents to allow the breezes to pass through; in winter, they leave the sides down.

In a large tent, the supports for the ridge pole are up to ten feet tall and six feet long, and the tent may stretch from thirty to forty feet. A loom often sits in the center of the tent. Storage boxes containing dress–up finery, saddles, bags of grain and rifles complete the room divider.

The women's domain – the kitchen and workroom – may vary in size depending on economic status, but it usually contains a low iron tripod for supporting cooking utensils over a campfire, fuel (sticks, grass, weeds or dried cow manure), cooking pots and a woven flat basket. Eating utensils are uncommon in a Berber's home – there'll be a soup bowl or two, maybe a spoon, and a flat tray for serving the meals. "Fingers were made before forks" works for most food, and one drinks soup from a bowl. If only one bowl is available, you take turns having supper, or you take a few sips and pass it to the next person.

Every tent has a shiny copper teakettle, a pewter or granite teapot and a few small tea glasses. On a sunny morning, you can see the reflection of the polished brass tray from a long distance.

The well is a community gathering place for getting the day's water supply and for doing laundry. Water–sellers circulate in the markets with goatskins of cool water slung across their shoulders. Goatskins hold water in the tents as well, unless the family owns a large water pot.

A second goatskin, supported by a tripod, serves as a churn. Poor women who can't afford the kneading crocks sold in the markets use the smooth side of a sheepskin as a kneading board. In the mountains one can buy a beautiful flat kneading bowl expertly carved from a huge piece of wood.

The hand mill is made from two round stones. Berber millstones are carved from roughly–hewn stone. They vary in size, from fifteen to eighteen inches in circumference, and they are shaped like a hamburger bun, with the two flat sides together and slightly hollowed to contain the grain. The bottom stone has a peg in the center to hold the two in place, and the top stone has a peg on the side. Two women usually sit on the ground, each grasping a peg to turn the stones.

Christian Roots

According to tradition, the Berbers of North Africa were Canaanites who fled from Joshua and his army when the children of Israel entered the Promised Land. Scholars have never proven this, nor have they come up with any better theory regarding their origin.

We know that the Berbers came from the east and are of the white race. Their language has some similarities to old Egyptian, old Libyan and Kurdish. Their name, Berber, comes from the Greek term "barbarians," meaning an uncivilized race that didn't speak Greek. Barbarossa (Redbeard) was a pirate who brought notoriety to the Barbary Coast in the sixteenth century, and his reputation probably expanded the meaning of the word *barbarian*.

Egyptians, Phoenicians, Greeks, Romans, Goths and Vandals touched the borders or settled on North African coasts. Berber Mauritania became a Roman province, turbulent and troublesome. An impressive Roman city, Volubilis, was not far from Meknes.

The Berbers hated the Roman yoke, so they saw the Arab armies as deliverers. Algerian Berbers formed the backbone of the Moorish invasion into Spain, where their leader, Tarik, left his name to the greatest fortress in the world: Gibraltar (in Arabic, "the mountain of Tarik"). Before long, the Berbers realized that one oppressor was as bad as another. They revolted, set up a kingdom of their own and fought the Arabs fiercely.

The desperate struggle in Algeria lasted twenty years. However, the Arabs finally crushed the rebellion, and the Muslim horde broke through the eastern border of Morocco. Tribe by tribe westward to the Atlantic, they met desperate uprisings and fierce battles.

Tradition maintains that the fierce Zemmour tribe of Khemisset was the last in Morocco to submit. Having conquered all the tribes in the country except one, the Arab chief sent the final threatening message to the leader of the Zemmours, "Witness to the prophet or die by the sword!" The Zemmours' response, as recorded by a French historian, was "We'll think about it." And, the historian adds, "They thought about it and came." The name of the clan surrounding Sunset

Farm confirms this historical account. The people are known as the *Khum-mu-ja*, which, said slowly and translated into English, becomes the "they–thought–about–it–and–came" tribe.

The Khummuja, who heard the gospel from the missionary pioneers preaching in the huge Tuesday market and then from Charles Fraser–Smith, vowed that no member of their tribe would ever become a Christian. GMU missionaries there won many friends but knew of very few who seemed to take their message seriously.

Tertullian, Origen and Augustine were outstanding North African churchmen and renowned Christian theologians and writers. All evidence points to the former existence of a strong Christian community among the Berbers, spread through personal witness and unflinching faith. Origen said, "The blood of the martyrs is the seed of the church." Yet a scant 400 years later, all who refused to submit to Islam were slaughtered for their faith, and with them, the North African church died.

It is appalling to realize that such a large, nominally Christian nation could be swept into total submission by a false religion. George Reed believed that the lack of a Bible translated into the Berber language led to their downfall. That belief explains why our early missionaries placed such a heavy emphasis on translating the Word.

The Berbers themselves are vaguely aware of their Christian roots, although they long ago forgot the meaning of the traces that remain. Some women don't spin their wool or work on their crafts on Sundays. Berbers weave the cross into their rugs, carve it on their saddles and display it on the gates to their villages, but no one understands its significance.

Would the priceless martyrs' seed of the North African church sprout and grow in our corner of the Muslim world? Or in our generation? Our knowledge of Berber history endeared these people to us. It also strengthened our belief that we could find gems among them who would become stalwarts of the faith.

Chapter 12

Our Berber Friends

My trusty bicycle took me to the Berber village of Mijjot regularly. When Don P. Shidler visited Meknes in 1947, he borrowed a bike and joined me on the fourteen–kilometer ride. We left Derb Skat and headed up the hill through the new city and finally hit open country on the hardtop road. It was a beautiful April day, with a clear blue sky and majestic snow–capped mountains before us, the fields a solid carpet of wildflowers dotted with red poppies. Mr. Shidler quipped that bicycling was fine in Morocco half the time: We traveled over rolling hills, a wonderful ride on the way down, but not so good when we peddled up the next one.

As we neared the village, we could see the cluster of Berber tents in the distance. The children I taught each week ran down to meet us. We went directly to the home of a Christian man, who cleared a spot for Mr. Shidler to sit on a clean grass mat. I knew this family would take good care of Mr. Shidler, so I left him and went to a neighboring tent, where I held a women's meeting. When the men showed up, I had a class for them. At last it was the children's turn. They had waited impatiently for their special class.

Meanwhile, Mr. Shidler had watched the man's wife prepare the meal. The tent contained two small millstones to make flour and cereal, several pots in one corner, an old teakettle, a teapot and a tray. The woman, with her baby on her knee, sat on the ground feeding a small grass fire as she prepared the meal of couscous with warm goat's milk poured on top.

Mr. Shidler and I, being guests, ate with the men. We formed a circle around the plate of food, took a small amount of couscous in our palms, rolled it into a ball and, as you would with a marble, shot it into our mouths. Mr. Shidler, though silently appalled, did his best to follow our instructions. He had a hard time finding his mouth! The women ate after we had finished.

The ride back to Meknes gave GMU's vice president time to reflect on the life of a missionary – pedaling twenty–eight kilometers, holding three services and tending to other matters back at the mission home, all in one day. When he became president a few years later, he was very considerate of the single women whom he had seen at work firsthand in many countries.

The day we rode to the village, Mr. Shidler also noticed the hard life of the Berber women. As he sat in that tent, he noticed several daughters around. Their father would give them in marriage at an early age for a dowry payment. Some became mothers at twelve or thirteen years of age. These girls lost their childhood quickly, becoming busy with the cares of motherhood and the drudgery of primitive household chores.

A Month with the Berbers

The people of the village begged me to come and stay with them. Finally, in 1950, it became possible. Mildred Swan, a British missionary, had joined GMU and lived with us at Derb Skat. Her heart with the Berbers, she was intent on learning their language. She knew she could accomplish this more easily by living among them. She was especially eager to start a school to teach the children.

When the Berbers invited us to spend a month with them, we decided to go. We borrowed a tent and collected cans of food, bath towels, toilet supplies, army cots, pillows, blankets, a primus stove, a radio and some handwork to do in our spare moments.

We had never pitched a tent before, and I don't know what we would have done if the Berber men had not come to give us a hand. After we had set up the cots with the mosquito nets over them, we decided to work out a toilet facility. The Berbers simply went out along the river, but we were too modest and western for that. We hung a curtain in the corner of the tent

Left: Derb Skat, the house that for years was the home of GMU missionaries and the centerpiece of many ministries. This photograph was taken looking up from the house's central courtyard. *Below:* "I have many sons and daughters in the faith who are very special to me," Ila Davis wrote.

Top: Frank C. Enyart, back, and Victor Swanson preach in a marketplace from the "Gospel Car," circa 1931.
Above: The family of Frank C. and Nellie Enyart with their guests at the Khemisset mission house, March 1925. From left: unknown, unknown, Judson Enyart, Mrs. Enyart, Ruthie Enyart, Mr. Enyart, Phebe Enyart, unknown, Freddie Enyart.
Right: Elizabeth Tryon (front) and Maude Cary (back, third from left) were two of many single missionaries who ministered during the early days of GMU's work in Morocco.

GMU missionaries Signe Johnson, Irene Wenholtz and Mary Mellinger inside Derb Skat, circa 1945. Miss Wenholtz and Miss Mellinger later left GMU to start an orphanage called Children's Haven.

Above: Meknes, May 1932: GMU missionaries met for worship with an assortment that included soldiers of the French Foreign Legion, Spanish believers and North American missionaries. Standing, second from the left, is Signe Johnson, and the tall man in the center of the back row is F.C. Enyart. The identities of the other individuals are uncertain.

Top: A water seller offers welcome relief to people before the Bab Mansour Gate in Meknes.
Above: Shopkeepers fry *svenge*, an unsweetened, raised doughnut eaten for breakfast or afternoon tea.
Right: Fortune-tellers whisper secrets in the Meknes market.

Above: Carrying bread through the streets of Meknes.
Left: A scene in the crowded street that runs past Derb Skat.

Below: Ila Marie Davis, center, was the second of four children.
Right: Ila with her parents, Wilhelmina (Minnie) Schultz Davis and Wilmer Newton Davis, in 1945. By February 1946, Ila would be in Morocco, far from her family's home in St. James, Minnesota.

Doris Schneider, Ila Davis and Verna Janz in Derb Skat with a children's class. The Schneider twins, two of Ila's special friends, are also pictured (left front and in Mrs. Schneider's arms).

Left: Ila Davis with a Berber family.
Below: Ila Davis loved Moroccan children, but she also loved the children of her co-workers. Here, she joins a lineup of missionary children.

Left: Ila included this photograph in one of her prayer letters. She wrote, "The picture was taken while camping among the Berbers this summer. The 'dolly' on my back welcomed us heartily and rather made her home in our tent."

The annual Festival of Sacrifice is an important holiday for Muslim families. "Everything is red with blood the day millions of sheep are slaughtered," wrote Ila Davis.

From the roof of Derb Skat, Ila Davis could see at least twenty minarets, towers from which the call to prayer went out five times a day.

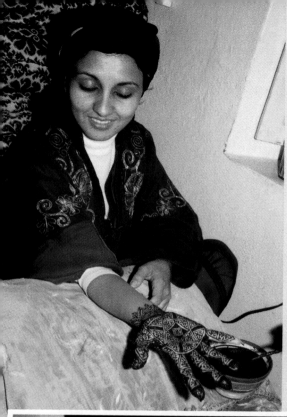

Left: Two days before a wedding, the hands and feet of a Moroccan bride are painted with henna in elaborate, lacy designs. *Below:* Moroccan custom decrees that a bride spend her wedding weekend dressing in one gorgeous garment after another.

Right: Sheikh Ali, a traveling Berber musician, in 1934. After a long struggle against the claims of the gospel, Sheikh Ali believed. "I could only sit down and laugh," he later said. "How simple it was!"

Below: Haddou, the Berber patriarch who believed in Christ as a child but did not hear the gospel again until about fifty years later.

Bottom: Christians from all over Morocco gathered for a national conference at Sunset Farm, May 1958.

This copy of a GMU Bible Correspondence Course flyer was printed in the largest daily Arabic journal in Morocco as a warning to students not to take the courses. Instead, more than thirty students cut out the threatening advertisement and sent it in to request the initial course.

Above: Eliyahu, a Jew; Abdallah, a Berber; and Mehdi, an Arab, represent the three Moroccan people groups to which GMU missionaries have taken the gospel.

Top right: Doris Schneider dispenses medicines to Berber neighbors from the first-aid station at Sunset Farm, near Khemisset.

Above right: Mildred Swan, center, pitched her tent beside the black goat-hair tents of her Berber friends, high in the Atlas Mountains.

Ila Davis in traditional Moroccan dress, 1979.

Some of Ila Davis' Soussi friends.

Ila found that ministry to Morocco's secluded women was especially difficult. And yet, "I found many jewels who rose above their small worlds," she wrote.

Young campers at Sunset Farm act out the story of Noah and the ark.

Workers prepare lunch during a church conference in Rabat

The 1963-64 class of missionary children at Bethel Academy, Tangier. With them are missionaries Irene Fisk (front row, right); Wilma Friesen (middle, left); Lois and Richard Clinesmith (middle, right); and Peter Z. Friesen (back, second from left). R.J. Reinmiller, who would become GMU's president in 1968, is at the left of the back row.

Left: Participants in GMU's 1955 field conference stand behind the chapel at Sunset Farm. Front: Stephen Jessup, Dan Jessup, Betty Eveland, Suzanne Schneider, Payne child, Lois Roth, Janet Payne, Mary Peterson, Verna Janz. Middle: Thomas Jessup, Raoma Jessup, Signe Johnson, Beulah Weston, Doris Schneider, Dorothea Payne, Ila Davis, Irma Peterson, Don Peterson. Back: Maynard Yoder, Karen Yoder, Margaret Yoder, Bob Schneider, GMU President Donald P. Shidler, Clem Payne, Mildred Swan, Elizabeth Speight, Marston Speight.
Below: Delores and Fred Plastow, left, and Peter and Wilma Friesen reach the port of Málaga, Spain, on Nov. 18, 1969, as part of GMU's evacuation from Morocco.

George Christian Weiss, former GMU president and missions director for Back to the Bible Broadcast, breaks ground for the first building of the Málaga Media Center in 1968. Watching, from left, are missionaries Marjorie Preston, Doris Schneider, Dorothea Payne, Clem Payne and Bob Schneider; Boushta Zerruk, a Moroccan; and Evelyn Weiss.

Above: Victor Swanson baptizes
Sheikh Ali, the traveling minstrel,
during an Easter Sunday service in
the early days of GMU ministry in
Morocco. Today, Moroccan
baptisms take place secretly, often
in a bathtub at home.

and put a chamber pot behind it. At night, while everyone slept, we emptied the pot.

Quarrels all around us awakened us early each morning. The men argued over whose turn it was to use the water for irrigation or whether someone had used it too long. They gave us the clock to time the flow of water to a certain man's property since he was often guilty of keeping it overtime. Quarrels were so common and fierce that often the *cadi* intervened, threatening offenders with time in jail.

Many children had swollen, infected eyes because of the many flies. Pharmacies in Morocco sold medicines without a prescription. With antibiotic salve and other first–aid items, we held a small clinic every morning. Mothers came from many kilometers away with their children to get medicine for the children's eyes.

Hassan was about thirteen years old, but he had never had a chance to go to school because he had to herd the cows and sheep every day. At night he joined his friends for a Bible lesson, but he wanted to learn to read for himself. During the day I followed him to the pasture. While he watched the animals, he learned the Arabic alphabet. He was so excited when he could form words by putting the letters together. Whenever Hassan saw me in later years, he thanked me again for teaching him to read. Learning Arabic made a big difference in his life.

I often went to the tent of one woman because I loved to watch her make bread. Every evening her husband filled the water jug at the spring. They kept the stone jar in the corner of the kitchen. She meticulously washed her hands and arms up to the elbows before beginning her task. After we ground the grain on the big stone mill, she scooped up the flour around the stone with her hands and prepared to knead the bread.

After the bread rose a little, she took it out to a homemade oven to bake. The oven, a round clay dome resembling a beehive, stood about four feet high. She built a fire on one side of it, leaving room for two loaves of bread to bake beside the fire. Bread was truly "the staff of life" to these tent people, who ate it with many glasses of hot, sweet mint tea.

The Festival of Sacrifice fell while we camped among the Berbers. Neither Mildred nor I had been in Morocco long, and we didn't know the customs of the country people. We didn't eat any breakfast the morning of the feast, thinking the people would entertain us all day. Early that morning the men put on their best white robes and went to an open space to pray in unison. They returned around eleven o'clock to butcher the sheep. Every family had a sheep, and every tent had a carcass hanging from a nearby tree.

When the butchering was done, some young folk walked into the city of Meknes. Almost all of the Berbers owned shoes, but they never wore them except in the city. On the way to the city, they carried their shoes on their heads to keep from wearing them out. People who did not go to town began to drop by to visit us that day, leaving the women to cut up the meat. We couldn't eat in front of guests, so by nightfall we were hungry.

Not wanting to make the same mistake on the second day, we ate a good, healthy breakfast. As we ate, our neighbors came in with a tray of food for us. As we ate our second breakfast, other neighbors came to invite us to share in their shish–ka–bob, made with the liver and fat of the animal. Soon others came, asking us to share the liver with them. That's how it was all day. Not wanting to offend anyone, we ate liver wrapped in fat countless times, washing it down with many glasses of sweet, hot mint tea. By evening both of us were sick.

We enjoyed our month with the tent people, though, and learned a great deal. We could easily imagine ourselves back in Abraham's time – with the easy pace and the primitive methods of cooking and farming. Their practical tents had probably not changed much over the thousands of years. When fleas, flies or filth became unbearable, they could move to a clean spot.

In later years, the country Berbers began to build small houses with corrugated tin roofs. The poorer people built small one-room houses, but the wealthy built beautiful houses elaborately decorated on the outside. Inside, however, they lived as they had in the tents. The Berbers were proud of their houses and glad to have keys. They felt much safer where wild animals, thieves and vandals couldn't get in.

Mildred and I talked about how fortunate these people were to live in the open, enjoying the warmth of the sunshine in the winter, the green grass and flowers in the spring and the cool breezes on hot summer afternoons. Yet how differently they looked at life! They envied the city people, remembering the mud after the rains and the cold winter nights when the wind drove the rain into the tents.

The world was small to these people. They could not fathom our descriptions of home. Mildred tried to tell the men where England was. "It is a small island in the middle of the ocean," she explained.

"Really!" exclaimed one Berber. "But where do they plow?"

Berbers Finding Christ

Missionaries recorded stories of Berbers who came to know Christ. The most colorful was of Sheikh Ali, who was born in a Berber village in southern Morocco, near Marrakech. He became a traveling musician, but no amount of success, popularity or money could erase the sin and fear of eternity that burdened his heart. When a friend told him about the message the foreigners preached in the Khemisset marketplace, he said, "That's what I'm looking for!"

When the missionaries came again, Sheikh Ali found a crowd gathered around them, laughing, mocking and cursing. He stood back and listened. "There, after living half a century in darkness," he later said, "I heard the gospel for the first time." He listened with respect every time the missionaries came, "but I was a Muslim, and of course my heart rebelled."

"God was working in my heart," he recounted. "In my hut, on the road, wherever I was, these thoughts filled my mind. I prayed to God to help me understand, and He did." Sheikh Ali reasoned that "if Jesus is the Word of God and a Spirit from

Him, then He is not a man as we are, and so our own book witnesses . . . He was born of the virgin Mary. All His works show they were God's works, not man's. Jesus was the Word of God and One from Him. He is God in the flesh! He is God's Son! And if so, He can save me!

"When I knew this, I could only sit down and laugh. How simple it was! How hard I had tried and failed! He has sent His Son and done it all."

Frank Shortridge, the missionary in Khemisset who recorded Sheikh Ali's testimony, lived in the Khemisset villa built by GMU about the time of Sheikh Ali's conversion. One night Shortridge passed Ali's room and heard the old musician singing a song he had composed:

> I am nothing, I have nothing,
> Neither house, nor land, nor money,
> Only a donkey.
> I am the Lord's and He is mine;
> He owns everything, all things are mine.
> Praise be to God! [1]

A little girl from Mijjot named Itto also became a Christian. She lived in a missionary's home for two years. Soon after my arrival in Morocco, the missionaries sent her back to her father's tent because of some misunderstanding. She shed many tears both before leaving and after arriving to live in the squalor and chaos of her father's tent. Because of extreme poverty and a large family, her father, a professing Christian, felt compelled to give Itto in marriage to a man with children older than she. When asked if Itto was happy, the father replied, "I don't know; sometimes she cries."

I saw Itto regularly. She was a beautiful girl even in her filthy, ragged garments. She had professed Christ while in the missionary's home, and she told me often that she was one of His.

From Arab to French Rule

French rule made life easier for the Berbers, eliminating much of the feuding, murders and sorrow and raising their economic level through jobs and education. However, after the French signed the 1912 treaty with the Arabs, they too had to fight their way, tribe by tribe, to gain control of Berber territory. No Sultan had ever set foot in Zemmour territory, but the French built the town of Khemisset and settled there.

When the French bombarded Sefrou, the terrified townspeople ran to Victor Swanson to beg his help. Swanson told them to raise a white flag atop the mosque tower and to carry another white flag of surrender as they went out to meet the enemy. He went with them, but since he did not speak French, the French scurried to find a soldier who spoke English to translate the negotiations.

In Meknes, officials also ran to the missionary, Frank Enyart. He advised giving the key to the city (which had a wall they locked at night and in times of danger) to the conquerors. He himself carried the key and delivered it to the French.

While the surrendering party negotiated at the main gate, the people began to escape from a gate on the opposite side of the city. With Enyart's help and trust, the French assured the people they would not harm them, nor would they confiscate their homes or possessions. Such conquerors the Berbers had never encountered, and they won their respect.

If you could visit Morocco today, you would find the Berbers of the plains and foothills still grazing their flocks and the mountain Berbers still dwelling in their huge homes of pounded earth. Ancient methods of farming and ancient nomadic tents still dot the landscape, and the hospitality, mint tea, fresh bread, couscous, shish-kebabs and fleas are still there. Antiquity is marching hand-in-hand with civilization into the twenty-first century.

[1]Elizabeth V. Tryon, *Morocco Now and Then* (Altoona, Penn.: Calvary Independent Church, date unknown).

Chapter 13

Young People Respond

In a village in southern Morocco, a young Arab studied English at the home of a British missionary. Missionaries had worked there for a long time. Now this station would be closed and the missionaries would move on because no one had responded to their message. About this time, Kareem began to show interest in the gospel. Then, by faith and with obvious joy, he accepted it.

He didn't know another Christian among his fellow countrymen until the missionary took him to the Christian summer camp at Sunset Farm. What a revelation this was to Kareem! Here he met dozens of Moroccans who had entered the Way and were living by the Word. Day after day he drank in the lessons with joy spread across his face and contentment in his heart. Now he knew the Word was the truth!

Kareem went back to his village and to his Muslim people. From childhood he had seen his friends ridicule the missionaries and throw stones at them. He had even seen them tear up a copy of the Gospel of John and set it on fire. But his newfound faith burned in his heart and he could not help sharing some of the delights of summer camp with his friends at school. Instead of rejoicing with him, they were shocked, and the persecution began. "If you don't denounce this heresy," they warned, "we will tell your father."

Kareem loved his family dearly and knew that to announce to his father that he had become a Christian would mean losing his family. Finally, he decided to deny it all. He wrote several letters to the missionaries and to people he had met at camp, telling them he would no longer follow Christ because the way was too hard. He asked them not to contact him by letter or in person ever again.

Eight months passed. Kareem moved to Casablanca to attend high school. Unexpectedly, he turned up one day at the door of a missionary who was praying for him. The first thing the missionary noticed was the absence of joy in Kareem's face, which had beamed the last time they had met. Kareem confessed that he was going through a severe mental strain and that perhaps he would need to see a doctor.

"It's not the doctor you need," the missionary told him. "It is Christ! We are getting a group ready to go to camp soon. We'd love to have you with us."

At the mention of camp, Kareem's face lit up. Remembering the camp he had attended and the blessings he had received, he agreed to return. We knew our prayers for him were not in vain.

Experience taught us that camps were not only a valuable witnessing and discipling ministry, but also a necessity. The two weeks of companionship and intense teaching could bring the previous year's work among children to fruition. For youngsters like Kareem, lone Christians in villages with no fellowship at all, camp acted as an elastic cord, pulling them back to the fold each time they fell away and strengthening their faith to keep a fall from happening again.

An Expanding Ministry

The first official camp was held at Sunset Farm in 1951, with six girls and two workers. In 1955 missionaries formed an inter-mission committee that drew children from all over Morocco and from all five evangelical organizations working in the country. The first boys' camp was held that year. It took a few seasons to get the camps running smoothly. We sent some early campers home because they caused problems and didn't understand the purpose of the camp. Soon no one wanted to risk having to leave this paradise of abundant food, exciting activities, fun classes and missionaries who loved them. One little girl broke her leg and spent some camp time in the Khemisset hospital. When the hospital released her, she begged to come back to camp.

By 1960 we were holding camps for six weeks each summer. More than 100 girls attended two camps (one for youngsters and the other for teens), and forty to sixty came for boys' camp. Camps grew even during the revolution and continued despite religious holidays. Sunset Farm expanded from a one-story farmhouse (quickly remodeled to a two-story), a thatch roof hut and a stable to a large camp and conference ground with a chapel, six military Quonset huts for cabins, a second missionary home and many other buildings.

When Charles Fraser-Smith owned the farm, he built a solid stone house with walls eighteen inches thick and a reinforced cement flat roof. Elsie Regier was the first GMU missionary to occupy the farm. She and the Spanish Christian couple living with her moved to the farm with a donkey cart early one Saturday morning. They found the three-room house damp and musty, totally uninhabitable. There were rats, scorpions, tarantulas and other less-threatening creatures that filled the day with screeches as they startled the women.

Fraser-Smith had sunk a deep well, reinforcing the walls to keep the sandy soil from collapsing. No one had used it for at least a decade except as a trash dump for the neighborhood tribes. Camp workers dropped a bucket with a long rope down the well, then hauled up the water and boiled it. When a well cleaner became available, he descended into the well and began sending up old buckets and trash of all kinds. As the Berber onlookers enjoyed the "entertainment," they claimed things they recognized as their own.

The well was deep enough to keep a large swimming pool and baptismal pool full after camps began. Although the water was clear and cool, it was not entirely pure. A generator eventually operated a pump and provided electricity during camps and conferences. We never had to use the rope and pail again.

It would be an understatement to say that summer was a busy time at Sunset Farm. I directed the girls' camps and helped as assistant cook and craft director at the first few boys' camps. Preparing the camp for the summer took weeks of hard labor for the Sunset Farm missionaries. Hammers pounded, needles flew and letters passed from station to station each spring as missionaries got ready. Spring housekeeping was the lot of whoever lived at the farm. Bob and Doris Schneider and Evelyn Stenbock spent most of their years in Morocco there, with Bob as director of the camps and conferences. Later Bob founded and directed the Arabic Bible correspondence course based at Sunset Farm.

Various missionary couples occupied the other house and managed the farm: Pete and Wilma Friesen, Al and Raoma Jessup and Rex and Lois Sandiford all put in long hours. If you asked any of them to describe missionary life, they would probably recall whitewashing ceilings, hoisting mattresses, painting – even varnishing a whole chapel full of church pews and making drapes for the chapel and other buildings.

The women made beds by the dozen; they sewed donated sheets to fit army cots donated from U.S. military salvage. Each event meant lugging out the beautiful handmade quilts donated by missionary societies back home – well-used over about sixteen seasons. And each event left a mountain of laundry to wash, dry, fold and return to storage – or, with camps back to back, to put back on the dozens of beds.

The activities that began to buzz at Sunset Farm each year amazed the tent-dwelling neighbors who were used to the stillness of the countryside. One youngster ran home crying, "Mama, Mama! You should see what's going on at the Americans' farm!" Berber children from the surrounding tents raided the garbage dump for treasures and lined up at the fence after dinner for leftovers to take to their families.

One boy – and only one – from the Khummuja tribe attended camp. He decided to come, and he worked hard to meet the requirements. Evelyn Stenbock arranged for him to come for a Bible lesson each week, and he learned the necessary Bible verses. There was one hitch, but he assured her it was no problem: He had to pay a fee of $2.60. Evelyn and Lois Sandiford were in the camp kitchen one of the last days of girls' camp when Rex walked in the door with little Hamid in tow. He had the money, all right – Rex had caught him in a cabin, going through other people's belongings to get it.

Hamid was reprimanded and then forgiven, and he broke the vow of the Khummuja by accepting Christ during camp.

Camps also meant learning to cook Moroccan-style food for large crowds. Campers had chores each day. They peeled vegetables and washed dishes. Summer is hot and dry in Morocco, and in Khemisset temperatures soared to as high as 120 degrees or more, with no air conditioning available. Kitchen duty for three meals a day, six weeks straight, was purely an act of love.

For many years, a remodeled stable served as our camp kitchen. We served meals outside under a huge bamboo roof in a picnic area. The children ate feast-like meals daily, typically meat-based stews with fresh bread, vegetables and fruit. In many homes they ate such food only on special occasions. As the camps grew, we bought huge amounts of meat, fresh vegetables and staples in nearby Khemisset. The first group of campers (only six children) was heard discussing the problem of a missionary killing a chicken for the meal. They couldn't eat chicken butchered by a non-Muslim. "But he prays, too," I heard one child remark. This satisfied the whole group, and they ate with delight.

The "cook's night off" allowed campers to prepare their own meals. Each group had its own campfire. The utensils designated for these meals became battered with use, and a few too many summer campouts brought some frying pans to an early death. The children in each group planned and prepared their entire meal, inviting any staff they wanted to share the meal with them. Arguments and serious quarrels always erupted, since meals vary in different parts of the country. The girls especially had definite ideas of how things should be done.

The bamboo-covered picnic yard was also used for evening meetings and for the biggest event of each camp – dramas. Moroccans are great actors. The children loved to dramatize Bible stories and other events to entertain us during the evening hours. Generally we had six cabins, and each presented their play on a different night. What work and planning went into these presentations! They designed elaborate costumes, beards and all. The people in Noah's time put on raucous parties, as did the people of Nineveh.

When they acted out the battle of Jericho, the walls really did fall down. The campers gathered objects, including metal tubs and pans, and piled them high to create the "wall." Around and around they marched, hooting and tooting their imaginary trumpets. As always, the delighted audience of close to eighty people laughed, clapped and shouted encouragement to the actors. At the proper moment, some children pushed the "wall" over with a huge clatter while "cymbals" crashed. The crowd went wild, and the Berbers for miles around must have wondered if the world was ending. Everyone participated in the plays with exuberance, holding nothing back. Timidity had no place on the stage.

I knew I had taken on an immense task when I decided to have the children put on a dramatized *Pilgrim's Progress*. The Lord helped me direct it. It was perhaps the greatest production of all. One girl carried a bundle on her back representing sin, which fell off as she approached the cross. Every camper participated with enthusiasm, and I am sure many truths of Christian living will remain with those girls the rest of their lives.

Fair Day was another big event at each camp. Each group planned a booth where they could display their projects or have a carnival stand. One special day, we separated the campers into pairs, each pair given material and the name of an animal they were to represent. I shall never forget the hilarious time we had as elephants, tigers, snakes and birds came up to enter the ark. One couple, posing as Noah and his wife, stood before a tent (the ark) and welcomed the animals.

Changed Lives

In 1961, I used the theme of "Calvary Love" in our morning workers' meeting at girls' camp. Love seemed to fill the camp. Great changes took place in the girls' lives. The proud became meek, the noisy became quiet, the troublemaker became a peacemaker. This was the result of good influence, the counseling of the workers, the work of the Word and prayer backing in the missionaries' homeland.

Often as I sat among young Moroccan ladies at camp, I thought of teenage American girls. These girls entertained us by the hour as we watched them create many different hairstyles. We arrived late for all scheduled activities because of it. We had learned long ago, however, not to hurry a young lady. Many profitable discussions took place during those hours of primping.

Vanity was not a problem with the younger girls. Young girls and boys preferred to collect the little green frogs so abundant at Sunset Farm. At one camp the missionaries had to wash several heads of thick black hair with kerosene, spending a whole afternoon trying to comb out the lice.

Naima, a high–school girl from Meknes, had attended camp before. Full of mischief, she wanted special attention. She was proud and felt herself a bit above the other girls. That year, as camp progressed, I heard Naima say, "I love my counselor, I love your counselor, I just love everybody!" We believed it when the time came for departure. The weeping and wailing reminded me of a Moroccan funeral. She kissed each girl half a dozen times and didn't leave anyone out. Some girls wept until they arrived home and probably cried for a long time after.

We soon found that boys' camps were quite different from girls' camps. We were thankful for our GMU men and for men from other missions who worked in the camps. They all had unique talents and were good disciplinarians, and the boys liked all of them. Some boys came to camp well–grounded in the Word, some not.

As a whole, the boys were much happier in camp than the girls. Perhaps their enjoyment of the scheduled activities stemmed from their lack of parental attention and their aimless days and nights on the streets at home. Boys were a nuisance to their mothers, who shooed them into the streets to play. Boys were spoiled: the girls had to work at home, but the boys did not. For them, kitchen duty was a pleasure. The cook talked and laughed with them while they grumbled over washing pots and pans. The boys got plenty of attention, and they ate it up.

One boy from Meknes who attended camp had, for most of the year, opposed the teaching that Christ died on the cross, but he told his counselor at camp that he believed. The boy asked for prayer during camp. Maynard Yoder, the missionary who knew the boy best, saw a new and changed lad.

Abdullah was only a small boy in size, but his intelligence and education made him seem much older than his thirteen years. He did not personally know any missionaries but had been reached through the Bible correspondence courses. He had finished studying the Gospel of Luke course by mail and professed faith in Christ before coming to camp. Since his knowledge of the Word came strictly through correspondence study, he preferred to sit with a counselor and learn more of the Word while other boys played or worked on crafts. It was a happy day for Abdullah when he and two other campers were baptized during the camp session. Taking a Christian name is not common among Moroccan believers. But Abdullah's great desire to study the Word and to preach to others made us understand why he wanted his name changed to Peter.

The counselors sometimes got tired of settling disputes and teaching campers the principles of basic Christian living, but they understood the importance of camp. One lad said, "If you had camp for twenty days instead of only ten days, we would all become Christians!" A fifteen–year–old boy told his seventeen–year–old friend, "I've been home only two hours, and already I wish I could return to camp, where there is no quarreling, no evil talk, no wickedness — and oh, to remain forever!" His companion answered, "Me, too!"

Chapter 14

'I Would Gather Children'

Children are precious to Moroccan parents. No matter how many children a mother has, she considers her new baby the most important of all. Parents don't seem to worry about the extra mouth to feed or where the money will come from for the seven–day feast. No one in the family seems jealous of the newcomer. Before the baby arrives, the mother begins to plan for the naming feast, making *zamata* (sweetened flour with almonds), cookies and cakes.

When the child is born, the father buys a sheep and butchers it the day before the naming feast. As he kills the sheep, he announces the child's name. Traditionally, the first son is named Muhammad, or a variation of the name; the first daughter is named Fatima, after the apostle's daughter. Modern parents have begun to choose new names, but I had as many as ten or twelve girls named Fatima in some of my classes.

Following the ancient custom, Moroccans wrap their babies in swaddling clothes at birth in the belief that a baby can't sleep without its hands bound to its body. The newcomer shares its mother's bed. No pacifiers are needed because the baby is comforted in its mother's arms and by its mother's breast.

Both fathers and mothers delight in their children. Fathers often carry their children, especially little girls, in the streets. They bounce and toss their babies in the air to gain a smile. The Moroccans' love for their little ones created a climate in which we could begin an effective outreach for Christ. We offered safe and happy learning experiences at classes in our home.

My first girls' class in Meknes averaged fifteen children a week – lively, giggling, curious girls, many of whom tagged along with friends, cousins or older sisters. Ours was an era of child evangelism, enthusiastically reaching out with love to teach the foundational truths of the gospel to any who would come to us. Besides the one-hour Bible lesson, songs and a memory verse, I set aside time to teach some of the girls to read. I used a small downstairs bedroom for the class.

Twice a week I had a boys' class. Bob Schneider practiced his Arabic lessons by keeping a record of the boys' names and teaching them a Bible verse. When they learned what we were teaching, some boys quit coming and began to taunt us in the street, calling us "blasphemers" or "infidels." Discipline in this class of rough-and-tumble boys was trying. Between classes the boys loved to knock at the door and then run away. Finally one day, I caught a child and paddled him, while his mother pleaded with me to stop. He became my best friend.

Children Hear the Gospel

My first years of ministry sped by quickly. The uncontrollable little girls I loved so much in spite of their shrill voices and continual stealing are probably grandmothers now. The horrible headaches that came when I attempted to teach them a simple memory verse were well worth it. Those children heard the gospel, and some of them accepted Jesus as their Savior. What about my prayer for a school in the country so the Berber girls could learn, too? The Lord used the revolution to bring education to all children. As a result, those little girls, whom many said could not learn, today carry briefcases and are the businesswomen of Morocco.

Children's ministry is always worthwhile. Every time a child entered our home for a class, I visualized what he or she might be in the future – a lawyer, a judge, a *cadi*, a teacher or even a minister in the government. Some of them could reach places of influence that might help us to reach the people for Christ or change the government's policy in our favor.

I made many mistakes when I began teaching Muslim children. In my Child Evangelism classes in America I could put my mind entirely on teaching. But in Morocco I had to be ever alert to the language. Even calling the roll in a class could be disastrous. During roll call one little boy continually repeated "Mkhaid," which a new missionary thought was his name. The boy was really trying to say that his name was "already registered."

The Muslims consider the Qur'an a holy book and never mistreat it. No one ever lies down in a room with his feet toward the Qur'an. Children, often outspoken, questioned my casual handling of my Holy Book. I learned not to lay it down carelessly, put it on the floor or cover it with papers, lest I suffer their rebuke. I often reminded my listeners that paper and ink are not important, but the message the book contains is what matters. The Bible is God's Holy Word, and I wanted to instill that truth deeply in their hearts.

Symbols of God, considered idols in their belief, were not at all acceptable. I quickly learned not to use pictures of Jesus when sharing the gospel. The boys I taught rebuked me, saying that they honored Jesus more than we missionaries did. The old object lesson of an egg – the shell, the white and the yolk – brought understanding the of Trinity, and I used it often. I learned, however, not to use the symbol of the cross in a picture or in jewelry. Moroccans accused us of worshiping the cross, and I wanted to prove that we didn't. It was my duty to teach the children that we worship God through Christ who reigns in our hearts.

Any boy or girl in Morocco could quote the Qur'anic verse, "He was not crucified nor was he killed, but another who resembled him was crucified in his place, and he ascended into heaven without death." In spite of this, the children in my classes never tired of hearing the story of the death and resurrection of Christ. They responded with delight when told that He did not remain in the grave. I loved to impart these truths to their hearts before they came to the questioning age. Many Moroccan men and women today believe Jesus died and rose from the dead, having tucked this truth in their hearts as little children.

Child Evangelism instructors in America encouraged teachers to present the Lord to the children as a great comforter during trouble. "You may not think a child has troubles," they said, "but they do. Their problems may be small to you, but not to them."

Over the years, I often remembered that comment. Everywhere I went, I saw brokenhearted children with no one to comfort them. Near our home, right in front of the mayor's office where prisoners stood trial, I often saw children pleading and weeping before the officers. Their pleas, however, were met with coldness. My heart wept with them and for them.

Vacation Bible Schools

When I learned the Arabic language, I began to hold Vacation Bible Schools for girls. You would have enjoyed peeking into Derb Skat's court at the scene. The little ones sat on a straw mat. Older girls sat on low, traditional couches behind them. And the biggest girls, the young teens who would soon be married, got the foreign chairs and benches. The little girls wore their black hair neatly combed into pigtails, and the older ones often had one shiny black braid down the back. Their eyes sparkled as they sang choruses translated into their own language: "One Door and Only One," "Joy, Joy, Joy" and, of course, "Jesus Loves Me."

The court became a beehive of activity during VBS. As many as sixty girls attended some summers, and for ten days they came regularly. They came to the door as early as 6:30 a.m. asking, "Is it time for school to begin?" We had little peace until we finally admitted them at about 8:30. Various missionaries helped with the schools each year, and as time went on, the older Christian girls began to take their places as helpers.

Each day began with a short devotional, a time of singing and a missionary story. At 9:15 we divided into classes. I often took the tots, Doris Schneider the middle group, and Phyllis Blake or Verna Janz the older children. We presented the plan of salvation day by day, and we thrilled to see their hearts open with understanding. We often saw girls ask Jesus to come into their hearts before the week ended.

Children with whom we already had contact, especially the girls who attended our regular classes, formed the core of our VBS group each year. When two girls failed to show up for class after school one Saturday, we began to worry. Their teacher at school had threatened them before, yet for a year and a half they had not missed a class for that reason.

Anxiously I awaited the next day, since these two sisters, jewels of our Savior, came regularly for the Sunday morning meeting. When they came, I sat with them at our breakfast table, and they explained their absence. The teacher had whipped one of them because she came to us, the "blasphemers." They ran home to tell their father. He rushed to the teacher and rudely told this educated, well–read Muslim that it was none of his business where the girls went after school. He frightened the teacher so much that the teacher never tried to keep them away again. Later the father asked me to continue "reading and praying" with his daughters.

After that, girls who had feared coming began to return. The VBS that year was one of the best. We had no opposition, and several girls accepted the Lord. This raised our attendance at the Sunday morning meeting for Christian girls to six lovely young women. Together we began to pray for them, as the next hurdle they would encounter would be marriage.

VBS always brought new children to our home. We invited their mothers to attend the closing program, which gave us contacts with new families. Whether I lived in Meknes, El Hajeb, Khemisset or Derb Skat, I always conducted VBS there and traveled to the other stations for VBS also. The idea of concentrated teaching in VBS for ten days became popular, and we saw early that VBS, like camp, was a ministry worth giving our full attention.

We didn't have any literature in the Moroccan dialect that we could use for the Vacation Bible Schools, so another missionary and I spent many hours translating material. We looked for pictures suitable for the children to color and for Arabic words they could understand. We translated two series of five lessons, one for smaller children and another for those who could read.

I believe the best way to reach Muslims is through children. They learn to love Jesus by the stories of His life long before they reach the questioning age. We could often reach the families of these children when they invited us to their homes. If you were to question believers in the fellowship meetings today, you would find that most of them became Christians as children.

An old poem sums up the path of ministry on which the Lord has led me. This ministry has been a wonderful part of a very happy life:

> Some would gather money along the path of life;
> Some would gather roses and rest from worldly strife.
> But I would gather children from among the thorns of sin;
> I would seek a little pigtail and a silly, toothless grin.
> For money cannot enter in that land of endless day,
> And roses that are gathered soon will wilt along the way.
> But oh, the laughing children, as I cross the Sunset Sea
> And the gates swing wide to heaven—
> I can take them in with me!

Chapter 15

All in a Day's Work

I stepped out the door of my home in Meknes one January morning, bundled in sweaters, raincoat and boots, ready to meet the weather. A strong wind drove the icy rain under the flaps in my coat and into my sleeves. Whipped and drenched by the storm, I rushed into the *derb* with one thought: to finish my errands and get back home soon.

Then I saw them, an elderly couple whose cardboard "home" sat just outside my door. The man slept comfortably, covered with the hood of his *jelaba* while his bare feet lay exposed to the weather. The woman gathered stray pieces of charcoal to make a fire.

A feeling of guilt swept through me as I remembered that even our Lord had no home. I thought too of the tragic condition of these who didn't know Christ. My occasional franc dropped in a beggar's bucket did precious little to alleviate the misery of so many impoverished people in the great city of Meknes. My concern and witness for Christ were insignificant drops in a great sea of souls. The sin, evil, deceit and unconcern that I witnessed day in and day out crushed my heart as I cried in all humility, "At any cost, Lord!"

Meknes and Khemisset

I moved back to Derb Skat in 1959 and lived there for the remainder of my time in Morocco. The eight years I lived in Khemisset hold many wonderful memories. While there, I commuted to Meknes frequently. The people in both places held a special place in my heart, and my mind churned with their problems, plans and prayer needs.

Khemisset was rapidly becoming a city, but it kept a small-town atmosphere, including widespread poverty and illiteracy. The second language in Meknes was French; the third, Shilha. In Khemisset it was the other way around: first

117

was Arabic; second, Shilha; third (and rarely), French. In Meknes I walked or biked; in Khemisset I rode a motor bike.

As a sideline in Meknes, I taught private English lessons to Moroccans. In Khemisset I took my turn teaching elementary school to missionary children. A schoolteacher soon relieved me of that duty. President Don Shidler had diverted a new recruit, Evelyn Stenbock, from language study in Switzerland and assigned her to teach missionary children in Morocco. He saw that our teaching the children distracted us from our main purpose in Morocco: evangelizing and teaching Moroccans. He also believed that our style of home schooling lacked the necessary discipline. Dorothea Payne was strict, but neither Doris Schneider nor I could be very tough. We accepted his decision, and I joined with the children's parents to instill respect in their minds for this new authority about to enter their lives. They would call her "Miss Stenbock," not "Aunt Evelyn." She lived with me at the Khemisset Girls' School but commuted by motorbike to Sunset Farm, where she set up a "real school" complete with the pledge of allegiance and recess. Evelyn was relieved of her teaching duties three years later when, in 1958, GMU opened Bethel Academy, a boarding school in Tangier for missionary children.

Growing up is inevitable. Chubby–faced little Vance Payne, my only Sunday School pupil when he was three, returned to the United States to attend high school. When they were fifteen, the Schneider twins, David and Daniel, and Vance Payne's little brother Dean also boarded a freighter in Casablanca, bound for high school in the U.S. A part of my heart followed the boys across the ocean, and I longed to hear they had arrived safely. I felt as if my own children were leaving home.

In Meknes I worked with many sophisticated men and women and increasingly with school girls and boys. Khemisset was different. You would have loved to attend a Sunday morning service in the outskirts of Khemisset in late winter. We sat in the doorway of a grass hut, making as much use of the sun's heat as possible. Grass–carpeted hills speckled with marigolds stretched out before us. Moulay Hamadi and his family sat on the ground as I did, feet tucked under us in Indian fashion, reading the Word of God.

Hamadi was proud of a new treasure he had obtained, a New Testament in colloquial Arabic. He called it his strength, the light of his life. I had taught him to read, and he read confidently, expounding the Word as he went along. There were many "ahs" and "ohs" from his congregation of his brother, mother, sister, wife, nephew and children. Occasionally a hen crept behind us to find a place in the hut to lay her egg.

One day Moulay Hamadi explained to me, "You are my only teacher, and I'm counting on you to help me!" Unemployed, he constantly dreamed of a job in faraway Casablanca. He promised, "Even if I get a job in Casablanca, I'll come back every Sunday for the meeting. I wouldn't miss it for anything!"

Moulay Hamadi's amazement the first time he attended the all-Morocco conference at Sunset Farm is difficult to imagine. He was a laborer unaccustomed to protocol and order. The only religious meeting Hamadi had ever attended was the little gathering at his grass hut. He had never heard a preacher, nor had he ever heard the joyful, melodious sounds of the piano, with more than a hundred voices singing God's praise. His testimony was a highlight that year because his life showed he accepted the Bible as God's Holy Word and zealously studied it. Hamadi often repeated, "I believe that Jesus died. I believe all that He has written in His Book. I believe, not because you have said it, but because I have read it for myself." One missionary exclaimed, "This is God's doing! Surround him with prayer that he might be preserved for the building of His church here in Morocco!"

Hamadi's nephew, Omar, came every day to my house in Khemisset. If he had been a girl, I'd have taken him in. Omar became a Christian as a little boy, and at fourteen he was a bright light for the Lord Jesus, simple and loving. He had a big smile that never went away. His IQ may not have been very high, but he had spiritual insight well beyond that of many adults.

Omar's mother was a temperamental woman with no compassion, not even for her own children. She sent Omar to the poorhouse to eat all his meals. One year he told her he would not fast Ramadan, and she warned him that she would "finish him off" if he didn't fast. I found odd jobs for him to do to earn money for camp and fed him when he needed it – which, with his lanky frame and long legs, was anytime I saw him!

Omar's sister attended the Khemisset Girl's School. The school was in the same building as my apartment, but with separate living quarters. We had built a stone privacy wall around the back yard, with a gate that locked. The girls' kitchen door opened into the yard, where there was a stone washhouse with a cement floor.

Aisha, a Christian girl who worked for the missionaries next door to me, often spent time with the students. One evening she and four other girls decided to heat up the washhouse with a charcoal pot and spend the evening in a *hammam* – their homemade sauna. Moroccan steam baths are famous for being very hot and lasting for hours. The door was closed to keep in the precious heat while the girls chattered, giggled and scrubbed away. Aisha, always the servant, stood over the charcoal pot dipping water and helping the other girls rinse their backs and wash their hair.

Suddenly, there was a frantic pounding on my door next to the garden gate. Hearing a woman screaming, Evelyn and I ran to see who it was. Omar's mother, outside the yard, was watching through the crack along the gate as the door to the bath opened and the girls, unclothed, staggered out.

We all raced through my apartment into the girls' quarters and out the door. I called the doctor while Evelyn and Omar's mother dragged and pulled the naked girls into the house, covered them and kept them from going to sleep. Aisha, who had been serving, had received the biggest dose of charcoal fumes. Evelyn slapped her cheeks until her hand was red, crying "Aisha, don't go to sleep! Aisha, Aisha! Don't go to sleep!" At the doctor's suggestion, I quickly made strong coffee, and when he arrived, we were forcing it down their throats.

We considered it a miracle that the girls were found – and by a mother not usually friendly but sent by God that night.

Constant Challenges

No matter where I lived, June, July and August always held activity, challenge, excitement and ministry, affecting children and teenagers from all over the country. Summer was evangelism time. The rest of the year, daily teaching and living out the gospel occupied our time. As I introduced a group of new missionaries to the Moroccan way of life, thought and culture, I realized I needed them to remind me of the American culture and standards I had left so many years before.

The people of Morocco and their needs utterly occupied my heart, soul and mind. From 6:30 in the morning until sometimes as late as 9:30 at night, I taught and discipled the people and prayed with them about the concerns on their hearts.

Life in such a busy place as Derb Skat seldom followed a routine. Each morning the Lord had a fresh list of opportunities prepared for me, and He often handed them to me one heart at a time. The prayers of my strong, supportive group of friends in the States surrounded me and carried me along. I knew I could count on them to hold a long, detailed list of burdens before God, who often answered in clear and remarkable ways.

Early teen marriages proved to be a major problem for the young women. As the girls confided in me, we prayed especially concerning this burden. Malika, who spent a week with me one Christmas, spoke for all girls her age when she spoke of the continual battle in her home over finding her a husband.

I asked for prayer for Malika's father, and to her and my delight, he joined his wife and two daughters for two days of the all–Morocco conference. When Malika heard we would hold a baptismal service, she begged to be baptized. She feared her parents' reaction, but she wanted to follow this command of Christ so much that she was willing to ask them for their consent. After much discussion and many tears, we finally decided to delay her baptism for a few months.

Such emotional moments are not in vain. I carefully explained the way of salvation and the meaning of baptism to Malika's father. I believe in the God of the impossible, who could use such a time of witness to draw these parents to Himself.

The Moroccan believers learned to pray with faith, believing that God would answer. And He did. One young woman, whose engagement struggles I will tell you about later, once exclaimed, "The Lord is working! I've seen things happen I would never have imagined." Such bursts of praise and expectancy cheered me up and carried me along during darker hours. As I watched my growing circle of believing friends struggle, learn, obey and grow, the Lord reassured me that if we missionaries had to leave, He would raise a witness for Himself from the Moroccan church.

Chapter 16

The End? Or the Beginning?

Many people have called Morocco a man's world. From my experience, though, I would call it a woman's world. Behind their meek and gentle facade, behind their veils and big, blanket-like cloaks, the women of Morocco are extremely powerful, domineering and aggressive. They often intimidated men both in the home and on the street.

To travel on intercity buses, people purchase either first- or second-class tickets. Women often buy second-class tickets, then crowd in ahead of the other passengers and occupy the first-class seats. No one, neither the ticket-holders nor the driver nor even the police, can move these women. They loudly proclaim that they will not change seats. No amount of shouting can embarrass them. Eventually the bus must leave, so the true ticket-holders give up and meekly move to the back of the bus.

One must feel sorry for the merchants who deal daily with such women. Women don't haggle with the merchants; they state their price and stick to it. The merchants, knowing they can't win, give in and sell for that price. The women coveted our used American-made clothing, but we had to almost give things away. Even when we sold an item at a ridiculously low price, we found the women skillfully driving a hard bargain.

Learning to Love the Women

Women were not interested in politics or religion. Only when they were old did friends shame them for not praying or going to the mosque and getting ready to die. Women didn't participate in school activities or neighborhood affairs. Their place was in the home, and some lived most of their lives in relative seclusion, going out only to weddings, circumcision feasts or the public bath. A woman's view of life could be very narrow since she lived in such a small world.

Many traveled only in a close-knit group, with the mother-in-law's sharp eye and ear always on them.

I was much more likely to trust a man in my home than a woman. Even women who loved us dearly took anything they could lay their hands on. If I left the room for a moment, my flannelgraph background disappeared. The last errand for many women was a trip to the bathroom, where they loaded up on bath towels or any other loose items. Fewer tea glasses returned to the kitchen for washing than we set out, and anything not nailed down was apt to disappear. We visited homes where we found our spoons, dishes, tea glasses, pictures and wash cloths. If we claimed any of these items, they shamed us for accusing them and made us look worse than the thief herself.

I suspected one girl who worked for me for a while of stealing, but I could never catch her in the act. One day I called at her home unexpectedly. I saw towels, toys, pictures, scissors and many other things, some of them belonging to missionaries who were on furlough and for whose possessions I was responsible. When I approached her later, she denied she had taken them. "Those are all mine," she claimed. I threatened to go with her to her home, but she pleaded with me not to go, promising to return everything. She returned only the things I had listed.

Once, I found a sugar cone in the hood of one woman's *jelaba*. She confessed to taking many things by saying, "Yes, I took those things to give to the poor so I could preach to them about Christ."

The talent that created the lies we heard could surely have invented some fantastic wonders if these women had channeled it in the right direction. One woman had several children out of wedlock, populating an orphanage. Once she admitted she was pregnant but declared that no human father was involved.

Moroccan women are very proud and extremely critical of one another. We could never hope to hold home Bible studies because the women feared other tongues too much. They criticized one another's homes, the housekeeping, the food and everything they saw, making the information they gathered the focal point of future gossip. Once when we held a Christmas party in our home in Meknes, one woman criticized the bread, the soup and the coffee, since they were not like hers. I was boiling with anger before she was done, and it helped me understand why most women didn't warm to the idea of inviting others into their homes.

And quarrels! One woman would say unkind things to another, true or untrue, and the other would loudly defend herself. Another might be accused of stealing; still another was jealous and wanted to make trouble or was vengeful because of past arguments. Sometimes in my home the quarreling became so violent I threatened to throw them out. Others hesitated to fight in our house, so they finished their argument in the street after class. When I introduced Thamia to Souad, I had no idea they already knew each other. They went into the street after class to finish a quarrel they had begun years before.

Education and employment opportunities began drawing many women out of their homes. Today, the "street population" has tripled. The narrow streets of the *medina* are so jammed with humanity that at prime shopping hours one can scarcely get through. Television, children and grandchildren have expanded the horizons of these secluded women.

I devoted many hours each week to women's ministry, in their homes and in mine. How could I love such obstinate women so much if not for God's love flowing through me? As I lived among them, I found many jewels who rose above their small worlds. They channeled their creativity into embroidery, weaving, cooking and creating happy homes for their families, despite a dingy, crowded environment. Many longed to learn but had no opportunity to do so. A visit from a missionary broke the boredom on a dreary afternoon. I often heard "Liela is here!" ringing through a household with enthusiastic yells.

Some of my warmest memories are of those visits. When I arrived at a home, the family ushered me into the living room, where I was buried in the comfort of many cushions. The hostess sat on a mat on the floor in front of me with the tea tray. Everyone in the house set aside embroidery, spinning or other chores to listen. As I opened my Bible and began to read, a hush would come over the group, and I could sense the Holy Spirit ministering through me.

I set aside certain afternoons each week to make the rounds to the homes of the women on my list – some I had known for decades, others I had met only recently. Many of these women became believers, and if it had not been for their unbelieving husbands, they would gladly have joined us at our women's meetings, conferences and fellowship groups.

Folding Our Tents

Early in 1967, we began to hear disturbing news of government interference in various places. It seemed the authorities were looking for sufficient reason to make us stop our activities. They considered us disloyal to the king, the religious head of state. We also felt an enemy attack in the area of personnel needs, leaving us in confusion. I felt a conflict of soul and cried out with the Psalmist, "All thy waves and thy billows have gone over me!" I reached out my hand to the Savior, who makes the storm be still. The turmoil was not over, though.

In April 1967, the government ordered the missionaries at Khemisset to cease all activities immediately. The only surprise was that the order had been so long in coming. Any ministry that had the goal of winning converts from Islam was unlawful. The Moroccan government had expressed concern at the growing amount of "proselytism" among its Muslim subjects. The government especially did not like the Bible Correspondence Courses, so Bob Schneider, founder and director of this effective ministry, moved the literature center out of Morocco. He found a choice location just outside Málaga, Spain, and the mission decided to move the correspondence-course office, print shop and related ministries to Málaga.

Still the pressure mounted. By 1969, not unlike the nomads we had learned to love so much, most of the missionaries had silently folded their tents and slipped away. All mission stations were closed except Derb Skat, and all personnel were reassigned or repatriated.

There is a distinct advantage to living so many years in one place. I knew Meknes, and Meknes knew me. The thick, windowless stone walls of Derb Skat could protect many secrets. Twenty years of daily contact with the community, with people going in and out of my home daily and freely, made no mystery of what I was doing. Whether it would be beneficial to the ministry or harmful we could not know, but we lived with the knowledge that few in the city had been untouched by seventy-five years of faithful preaching of the Word in and around Meknes.

God had emissaries in high places. The little bookstall had grown to an impressive new bookstore where we shared the gospel with professionals. The vibrant window displays carried an open witness through banners and a wide selection of evangelical literature and Bibles in various languages. Maynard Yoder, the bookstore manager, held lectures in the bookstore that many people attended.

No one needed to brief the mayor of Meknes on the activities, message or purpose of the *Nsara* who operated the bookstore. Neither did anyone have to tell him the mission of the women in the *medina* whose love for children and young people had touched many of their own lives. When many missionaries were receiving the dreaded notice to leave the country immediately, Maynard was called to the mayor's office, where an official he knew met him.

"I have eaten in your home," said the caliph, "and you have eaten in mine." Having thus set the informal, friendly tone of the meeting, the two men discussed the current political climate. The official asked about me. Maynard told him I was living alone in my home in the *medina*. The meeting ended on a cordial note, and neither the Yoders nor I ever received an expulsion notice.

It was a stressful time. First the government closed the farm, banning any more activities there. The news staggered me because I had based my whole summer program on using the farm. It was hard to imagine life without that beautiful and well-equipped location for our camps and retreats. We had no other place to hold a baptism. And when I heard the government had closed the station in Sefrou – perhaps one of the most encouraging places in Morocco – I was stunned. There were young fellows in Sefrou ready to do their best to meet together, but my heart went out to the women there. I didn't know what they would do with no missionary to guide them.

The Future of the Moroccan Church

Many questions plagued us. How would the Moroccan church stay alive? Could it grow "underground"? Where could believers meet? Who would lead them? What about the women who heard the gospel only in the seclusion of their own homes? Even for women who did go out of the house, social customs made joint meetings with both men and women difficult, even with a missionary present. Without one, such meetings seemed impossible.

What about the future? What about me? The authorities had not expelled me. My mind toyed with solutions for myself. A few of the young people knew what was going on, but for the most part, we went on with our daily activities as if nothing had happened anywhere. I thought of taking an early furlough and then returning to a rented apartment. Hundreds of homes were open to me. There was the exciting possibility of new contacts through English classes, and I could teach those with no obligation to the government. I even thought about opening a mission station in neighboring Algeria and returning to Morocco when things cooled down.

It would have been a tragedy to give up Derb Skat, though. It was so well known in the city. As doors closed slowly around us, I could only cling to God's promises. We had no opposition, but in the back of our minds was the possibility that we would be next on the agenda. Some British missionaries signed an agreement not to preach the gospel, preferring to stay and be silent rather than to abandon their posts. I didn't know what I would do if the authorities asked me to sign such a paper.

Surely I could not make decisions as big as these alone. I would have to leave it with the Lord and trust Him to provide the wisdom and courage to act in His will when the time came.

In 1969, a young fellow from another city attended some special meetings at Derb Skat. "I was standing near the school," he reported, "when the police came and took me to the bureau. They tried to get me to say that the foreigners were still holding meetings in their home."

"This is getting closer to us," murmured one of our lads.

"But we can't let Satan have the victory," said one girl when she heard about the report. She rebuked me for not going ahead with the summer calendar of events. At her insistence, I arranged for the usual training session for her and other Moroccan workers.

The Yoders took their turn as house parents at the missionary children's school, eventually leaving Morocco to join the Málaga team. I had planned to leave on furlough that September, but the couple coming to take over during my absence were expelled from the country. I decided to take my furlough as planned but to come back within six months so I could keep my permanent visa. Except for meetings, Derb Skat would be closed. Meanwhile, summer activities – maybe the last we could ever have – had to go on. I had Vacation Bible Schools to conduct, a women's retreat planned with nowhere to hold it other than my own home and the regular schedule of camps to carry on somewhere and somehow.

When the summer ministries were over in 1969, I closed Derb Skat and took a six-month furlough as planned. Bob and Doris Schneider were living in Spain, where Bob had opened

Málaga Media Center. On my return trip to Morocco, I flew to Spain on March 28, 1970, wondering what might await me at the Moroccan border. A few days later, the Schneiders drove me into Morocco and home.

We had no trouble at the border. Following the recommendations of others, I entered on a tourist visa. This required me to leave the country after three months, with the threat of difficulty in returning after I left. Finding the Lord's plan for obtaining a new permanent visa was the uppermost concern in my mind.

The Schneiders returned to their home in Spain, and like Elijah, I felt that "I, only I" was left. I awoke every day with a feeling of urgency about the work. Some days ended with a sense of defeat, but looking back over each week, I saw an unusual confidence and love among the believers. They showed a great desire to live and walk in holiness before the Lord, with a longing to see others saved. One said, "I don't want to spend eternity without my family!" The tears she shed when she prayed showed her sincerity.

After two or three "vacations" in Europe with no indication of trouble at the border or in my work, I applied for a permanent visa. I waited almost two years before I got it. Meanwhile, the ministry continued. I had VBS workers to train, lessons to prepare and handwork projects to complete. The young men were busy with a Bible study on their own, led by a fine young Moroccan. We held monthly meetings with believers from around the country, one month in Meknes and every other month in places like Casablanca, Tangier and the mountains. It was good for our Meknes group to get away where they could relax and feel free from the possible watching eyes at home.

Christ was building His church, and the gates of hell could not prevail against it!

Chapter 17

Bargaining for a Bride

A little girl with a very big problem lived in a house in our *derb*. This immense problem stemmed from the fact that she came from a Muslim home and had become a Christian.

Hania and her brothers had attended classes at Derb Skat occasionally when they were small. As they got older, they sometimes joined the crowd stoning our door or cursing those who knocked to come in. Hania sometimes frightened new girls away by telling them that we butchered little girls.

However, Hania had heard the Word of God and memorized many verses. Although she appeared to oppose us, she did not forget what she had learned. She stood at the door of her home and wistfully watched as other girls came and went. In time she learned which girls were Christians, and by keeping an eye on the activity at our door, she knew the hours they came to class. One day as I returned home, Hania stopped me to ask if she could come Sunday with the Christian girls.

Hania was no stranger to me. This was our troublesome neighbor child, the one who had decided we were infidels and had done all she could to frighten other children away. We knew about the clever antics of bright adolescents like her. They would convince a foreigner of their sincerity for some personal gain – an open door for stealing, a chance to spy on the Christians to gain popularity in their own crowd, or even the hope of becoming teacher's pet, with unimaginable benefits. I knew Hania quite well, and I thought she was out to obtain some profit for herself or gather information that might harm the other girls. I did not allow her in.

Stumped on that try, Hania's determination grew. She became friends with one girl who came regularly to classes, and that friendship overruled my previous judgment. She had one foot in the door.

One day Hania plucked up her courage, reached up and grabbed the big brass knocker and banged hard. I poked my head out the *ashkoon* window on the second floor and said to her, "It's not time for class, Hania."

"I know!" She had moved back from the door and even then had to tilt her head back to see me. I decided to go down and let her in. After we sat, she said, "Other girls come Sunday mornings. Why can't I come then? Can I come, too?"

"The girls coming Sunday morning are Christians," I explained. "The only reason they come is to study the Word of God."

"But I want to study the Word of God! That's why I want to join them!" she insisted, and to back up her statement, she began to quote verses that she had learned when she was a little girl several years before.

My doubts were disappearing. With a prayer for wisdom, I opened the Bible and began to explain the gospel. Never did I have a better audience or a more Spirit-opened mind. Hania was ready to accept the Christ of the cross, and with Him, His cross. Hania had been a part of the crowd that persecuted those who believed. She understood what her lot would be if she confessed Jesus Christ as her Savior. Well aware of the consequences, she prayed and asked Him to save her.

From the first moment, my heart told me she was sincere. When her mother saw a big change and reported it to me, my hopes were confirmed. Educated in a Muslim school, she could read Arabic well and soon fell in love with the Bible. The other girls accepted her into the group; soon she was baptized. Hania had a close relationship with her mother. She prayed and longed for her to accept Christ, too. The Lord blessed her testimony; her mother was open to the gospel, which spared Hania from persecution in her home.

Whom Will They Marry?

Then came the big problem – one which comes to all young Moroccan girls. Hania was not the first girl to rebel against a system that called her to give up her childhood to marry. The price she would pay for marriage was great – she would have to give up her freedom for seclusion, marry a stranger, be ruled by a mother–in–law she had never met and be homesick or hated by other women in the home. At age twelve or thirteen – fourteen if a girl is lucky – the request for her comes. In the best scenario, a doting father or mother listens to her objections and tries to satisfy her wishes. But the reality of negotiations is all too painful; sometimes, even with the best of intentions, the parents overlook the girl's desires and she loses.

Like any girl her age, Hania understood marriage customs very well. Whether she wanted the man or not, whether she even knew him or not, she had to go to him like a slave to her new master's home. The problem was even more devastating to a Christian girl in a Muslim home. The marriage could mean new rules putting a stop to her meeting attendance and her friendships with missionaries and Moroccan Christians. Her new family could even persecute her for her Christian faith.

One day Hania came to me crying. Someone had come to her family to ask for her in marriage for their son. The first meeting between the parents had been a success. They would settle the agreement in a week.

What could we do? We covenanted to fast and pray, and Hania, rather than give up, asked me to join her in an appeal to her mother. Her mother, impressed with the change in her attitude since she had become a Christian, gave in to her pleading. She interceded for Hania, stopping the engagement plans. Hania would marry only a Christian like herself.

"Just bring one to us, Liela," said the mother.

Suddenly I was thrust into a matchmaker role. Find a suitable young Christian man for Hania? I couldn't think of a single young man then, so we dropped the subject, relieved that the matter was over.

If there is romance in the marriage game, it is both sets of parents who share it. A few weeks later, you might have seen Ali and Naima, the parents of another prospective groom for

Hania, walking through the narrow streets of Meknes. The long, silky skirts under Naima's *jelaba* swished as she followed six steps behind her husband. She carried a heavy basket on her head, while Ali and a boy he had hired carried additional baskets, one in each hand. Turning into an alley, they approached a heavy wooden door well-studded with brass nails. The brass knocker on the door was shaped like a hand, said to be the hand of Fatima, the prophet's daughter.

Ali heaved a sigh as he set down his heavy load. He lifted the brass hand twice, dropping it each time with a loud thud. The host, Ahmed, was waiting. He flung open the door with a hearty welcome for these treasured guests. His wife stood back in the court smiling with pride. The men had arranged everything, while she had worked hard to make this a flawless evening. Ali presented the baskets to the owner of the house. Hania's parents greeted them with salaams, good wishes, inquiries about their relatives' health, polite handshakes and kisses, the common greetings of the land.

The gift that filled so many baskets was sugar – four-pound cones wrapped in dark-blue paper, purchased from the local grocer. Moroccans never make sweet mint tea with *saneeda* (granulated sugar). Ah, no! Even the poor buy cone sugar, purchased from cones broken by the grocer to sell in small pieces. Those not so poor buy the whole cone. As part of the tea ritual, the host taps the cone with a tea glass in the right place with enough force to break the cone but not the glass. Twenty cones of sugar was an acceptable gift for the hostess on this occasion.

The guests hoped to barter for a daughter-in-law; the hosts wanted to be sure the son-in-law they gained was acceptable. Arranging a marriage for their offspring was a high point in their lives. The goal of this first meeting was for both families to be compatible so they could reach a mutually satisfying agreement. Although the stress level was high, both couples disguised their nervous excitement with gracious words and flattering chatter.

Naima followed Saadia, Hania's mother, to a beautifully kept parlor, with deep handmade carpets on the floor, plush covers over the soft wool cushions and enough pillows on each couch to lose a person. The men headed for a second living room. A multi-course meal was served in both rooms. Conversation was light, and tea was poured ceremoniously repeatedly. In a typically feminine atmosphere, the women joined in casual conversation while looking each another over. Saadia and the other women of the household made note of the smallest details. This was a potential mother-in-law. Was she sarcastic? Was she haughty? Was her manner genuine, or was this a mere facade she would remove once the honeymoon ended? Did her son have other wives? Did he have a job to support his family? Did he drink? Did he pray?

The real action is always in the room where the men meet, and once they strike a deal, it is set in stone.

"I hear you have a daughter of marriageable age." Ali spoke softly, turning to the purpose of the invitation.

"I do have," answered Ahmed.

"Would you take 20,000 *dirhams* for her?" asked Ali.

Ahmed sounded insulted as he shouted back, "Twenty thousand? Why, that wouldn't even buy wool for the mattresses! I demand 75,000 for her!"

A sweet young girl is worth seventy-five times 75,000 *dirhams*! Ahmed considered his own daughter priceless. Ali was not moved, though. "That is entirely too much," he said, and the bargaining was over for the night.

Today's engagements differ because women can attend coeducational schools, participate in sports and otherwise appear in public, where a couple can meet and even fall in love. In such cases, the young man tells his mother about the girl he wants to marry; she tells her mother about him. Miraculously, the fathers get together and settle the matter. Although the two young people know each other, the engagement proceeds in the traditional manner as if they did not.

Marriages cannot be made without the parents' consent. Today, as for centuries, most parents give their daughter to the first satisfactory family that asks for her and guarantees enough cash. The father is responsible for finding a husband for his daughter; allowing her to remain single would be shameful. Moroccans pitied those of us missionaries who were single.

Extended family and tribal ties can be very binding. If the father of the prospective groom happens to be a relative, even the most doting father may go back on his promise to his daughter; he cannot insult a relative by refusing him.

After Ali's third visit to Ahmed's home – and many more cones of sugar – the fathers set the final price at 50,000 *dirhams*.

Hania came running to me, saying this family had come to ask for her. They were still there. After they left, I marched over to the house, Hania at my side.

"Why did you allow this to happen?" I rebuked her mother. "You made a promise to me that Hania would marry only a Christian like herself."

"I asked you to bring a believer in Christ and you didn't," she said simply. "We are not children. I have given my word, and it must be so."

Customs or Happiness?

A new law in Morocco legally allowed a girl to accept or refuse a marriage. After the bargaining, but before the paper was signed, the *cadi* would go to the girl's home and ask her to give her consent or refusal to the proposal. The law was timely and progressive; it gave women who previously had no rights the freedom to say no. Sadly, old customs die hard. Rarely would a girl object to her father's decision.

While her parents served the *cadi* a beautiful meal, Hania rehearsed how she would tell him no when he approached her. She would explain that she was a Christian and the young man, a Muslim; they would not be compatible as man and wife. But when her father stepped through the door with the *cadi*, she froze. She had not known he would come too. Kindly but formally, the *cadi* asked for her decision. She stared at the floor and didn't say a word. He took her silence for approval. Later, weeping uncontrollably, Hania poured out the story to me. She did not want this marriage to an unbeliever, but she hadn't had the courage to speak up.

If the families are relatives or longtime friends, they may postpone signing the marriage contract, sometimes waiting until the wedding feast a year or more later. Even so, the agreement of the fathers stands as a binding vow. Other families sign the marriage contract in the presence of the *cadi* during the engagement visit.

After the engagement, whether through the father's verbal promise or the actual signing of the contract, the girl becomes the property of the man she will marry. She cannot travel or visit without his consent. If the wedding is delayed, each year her fiance must provide his bride with a sheep for the Big Feast. He gives her gifts of gold for other Muslim holidays. Breaking the engagement is tantamount to divorce. If she breaks the engagement, she returns all the money and gifts her fiance has given her. If he breaks the engagement, she keeps them.

I found the Christmas story in Matthew easier to understand once I realized the seriousness of Middle Eastern engagements. The marriage contract between Joseph and Mary had been signed. Although the wedding had not taken place, he would have had to file for divorce to free himself from obligations to her.

So Hania was engaged. Time went by. One day when she was out with her mother, her mother greeted a young man. "Who is he?" whispered Hania after the encounter. "That's the man you're going to marry," her mother answered.

I can only imagine the feelings of this young woman when she realized she had seen the man she was to marry. Suddenly the reality of the situation smothered her. Girls never communicated with young men then, even if they were betrothed. In desperation Hania wrote a letter to her fiance and asked me to read it. She intended to have her brother deliver it to the man at his shop. It was a last–resort effort in which Hania explained that she was a Christian and that if he wished, he could divorce her now that he knew this.

That night we heard terrible confusion next door. The groom's mother learned of the letter; the groom vowed he would marry Hania "even if she were a Jewess." Hania was badly beaten. When she could get away, she ran to show me the many welts on her back. Her scheme had failed; the marriage plans would go on.

Thus ended my first attempt to save a Christian girl from a marriage she didn't want. Feeling I had failed, I decided to learn more about Moroccan customs and develop a strong community of young believers to broaden the matrimonial choices for Christian youth.

Chapter 18

Wedding Bells, Moroccan Style

Many years have passed since Hania's wedding. I have known many young women who went through similar struggles, only to lose to the power of custom and marry against their will. I cannot imagine planning a big wedding as they must do, their hearts heavy because they want nothing to do with the result. Weddings in Morocco are huge, ceremonious events, often attended by the whole community. The dowry payment by the groom's family is only part of the bargain; the bride must prepare her trousseau.

One of Morocco's most beautiful crafts is double–sided embroidery, leaving an item reversible with no wrong side. The work is next to perfect – tiny stitches embroidered into intricate patterns by counting the threads. Not perfect, of course. Any Moroccan will tell you that "only God is perfect." Workmen deliberately break the pattern in a tile floor – preferably behind a closet door or in some other inconspicuous place – as an acknowledgment that "only God is perfect." The gorgeous embroidery girls and women do will doubtless also have a deliberate flaw somewhere, perhaps known only to the person who did it.

Preparing for the Marriage

The bride buys material for huge bed sheets. She begins to embroider the sheet two or three feet from the top in solid reversible embroidery. With all the sheets, pillows and booster pillows she has to embroider, the awesome task takes a year or more to finish. If the bride can't embroider, she can hire experts to do it for her. Since the community judges her by the number of sheets she brings in her trousseau, she will doubtless find help embroidering some of them. When multi–stitch portable sewing machines came to Morocco, the women were quick to obtain them. Machine embroidery, although not of the same quality as handwork, augments the punch needles and hand embroidery.

The bride also prepares several tablecloths, napkins, tea-tray covers and gifts for the groom's family, all of which she makes by hand.

Supposedly, the dowry money provides the many items the bride must have. As the wedding approaches, the family buys wool, washing and drying it and stuffing it into mattress covers they have made. The groom buys the wooden frames for the couches, and the mattresses must fit the frames, which must fit into his house. When finished, the frames and mattresses line the walls of the main room of the house, something like a big sectional sofa. The dream of every bride's mother is to send heavy velvet material woven with gold as covers for her daughter's couches. She makes a second set of covers for everyday use from washable flowered material.

Moroccans did not throw bridal showers or give wedding gifts while I was there. The bride had to buy her pots and pans, dishes and anything else she might need.

An Elaborate Affair

Weddings take place on the weekend, which begins on Friday, the holy day. On Thursday of the wedding, small boys hired by the family march the bride's belongings through the street to the groom's home, allowing the whole community to see how well prepared she is. The boys often carry the things piece by piece to show them off in the best possible manner.

Viewers of such a wedding procession are not casual onlookers. They will often examine the material to see if it is a good grade. The bride's family takes the bed and wardrobe apart and each carrier carries a few pieces. With some carrying only a few cushions, the procession may be very long. One bride had so many belongings that the first group was entering the groom's home while the last group was just leaving the bride's.

If the groom lives in another city, he will send a truck to haul the belongings to his home. A friend or relative accompanies the bridal outfit and remains with the goods until the bride arrives to make sure no one steals anything.

On Thursday night of the wedding weekend, the bride goes to the public bath. Her female relatives and close friends scrub her thoroughly and shave off any body hair. Later, when they return to the bride's home, the music begins and each woman does her version of the belly dance. The men from the wedding party celebrate in the groom's home, so the dances are for the women's own entertainment. Fat or thin, young or old, the women, forgetting themselves, tie a scarf around their long loose dresses to show the movements of their bodies. Each woman dances alone, her hands held up over her head as she looks down, mesmerized by the music and the rhythm of her body.

The groom donates henna leaves for the bride, which are boiled, drained, mixed with olive oil and made into a paste. On Friday, the bride sits patiently while a henna expert paints a delicate, lacy design on her hands and feet with a syringe or a toothpick. When the job is done she dries her hands and feet over a charcoal pot before wrapping and covering them with scarves specially embroidered for the occasion. The next morning the bride removes the scarves and washes off the mud pack. Her hands and feet look as though they have been fitted with dark lace gloves and socks.

The cooking begins on Saturday – on the roof, in a tent or even in a borrowed house if their own won't hold the immense crowd sure to come. They may have butchered fifty to 100 chickens, a cow or a sheep the day before, sometimes doing the butchering in the court, with the women watching and screaming and the drums rolling. They buy dozens of cases of bottled soft drinks and fresh bread from the bakery. Catering a wedding is an immense job!

Years ago women, with their drums, provided the only music at weddings. Now, however, groups of men calling themselves orchestras hire out for city weddings. They usually have an electric organ, guitars, violins, drums and an electric sound system.

Throughout the weekend, while the guests are partying, the bride sits in a room by herself, dressed in gorgeous clothes brought in by wedding experts. Each time she changes caftans, the hired wedding experts parade her in the court so the women can "ooh" and "aah" over her garments. This reminds the guests that they, too, should change, so they slip away to do so. Everyone wants her picture taken with the bride, and the guests often invited me to take the pictures.

The bride is placed in a tub–like contraption, dressed in all her finery, and is lifted to the shoulders of the women hired to provide her rented clothes. As they precariously hold their bridal burden high above their heads, they seem to fall into a trance, doing a muscle–straining belly dance.

I should point out that customs vary. The missionaries generally came at the close of the festivities and accompanied the bride to the groom's home, or waited with the groom if they were his guests.

At dawn on Sunday morning, the bride appears in her last outfit. Traditionally the bride and groom meet at the marriage bed. In today's changing world, weddings combine tradition with a few western customs. I have seen the groom with the bride (who wore a wedding dress with veil and train) while she cut a wedding cake and they fed each other a bite.

The bride is carried through the streets, where dancing and music awaken the city during the wedding march through town. Windows and doors open as sleepy people peer into the darkness to see who is going by.

When the members of the bridal party arrive at the groom's house, they usher the bride into the bedroom. Music fills the house and guests clap loudly to the beat of the drums as the marriage is consummated. To prove the bride's virginity, the groom throws her bloodstained *serwelle* (bloomers) into the court; a chicken is tied nearby, ready to be butchered if need be. As cultures blend, Moroccans have begun to omit customs such as this one from the ceremony.

A Dilemma for Christians

Most of the weddings of Christian young people I attended were mixed marriages. Often families forced a Christian to marry a Muslim. Yet I once witnessed the joyful occasion of a marriage of two believers. The customs practiced differed some because the couple came from a Berber village. Friends of the groom paraded him around town on a horse. They placed henna on the bride's head and broke a raw egg on top to ensure a fruitful womb.

We had a midnight meal with the groom in the room where the bride's trousseau had been brought a few days earlier. A commotion interrupted our meal. A friend of the groom opened the door and, carrying the bride on his back, dumped her on the bed. We finished our meal before holding a special Christian marriage ceremony for the couple.

Independence in Morocco brought some radical changes in marriage customs. The new law that stated a girl could not be married against her will also set the minimum age for marriage at sixteen. I was encouraged when the government passed these laws, but I soon learned people would rather disobey the law than break with tradition.

A missionary from a distant village in the Atlas Mountains asked if I knew a Christian girl who would marry a Christian barber in a mountain village. I went over my list of young ladies. One older girl investigated the possibility, but decided she couldn't endure village life. She also doubted she could be happy living on his meager earnings. I thought about suggesting Touria, a sweet young Christian girl, but she was barely old enough to attend teen camp.

The father of the barber was getting impatient. His son was twenty-one, and men married at a young age in his community. The father was pressuring the young Christian man to marry one of the little girls he had chosen for him.

When I returned home from my summer activities, I was shocked to learn that Touria's family had married her to a Muslim teacher in a mountain village. He had promised $200 for her. The family had served the dates and milk, sealing the deal. I later heard that the Christian barber could not resist his father's will and married a young woman of his village.

I remember well the wedding of a Christian girl who had her engagement party just a week before the wedding. While we were there, gifts from the groom arrived. He sent a large tray of henna leaves covered with many eggs, material for party dresses, shoes and gold jewelry. He also sent a live sheep, which was whisked away to the kitchen so the odor wouldn't offend the women.

A week later we sat at the wedding feast and waited for the bride to arrive. She had gone to the beauty parlor and didn't arrive until after the midnight meal had ended. The transformed woman looked like Cleopatra. She began changing into various outfits for the photographs with her many friends and family.

Samara, a teacher in a secondary school, married a believer and held the wedding in our home. She tried to cut out some customs because she had only her grandfather, a mosque teacher, to help with expenses.

Samara decided to forego the henna, orchestra and women hired to dress her. But her mother's friends would not allow such economizing. "This is your only daughter," they declared to Samara's mother. "Everything must be done according to custom! No woman can go to her husband without henna on her hands!"

I took this bride to the beauty parlor the day of the wedding. She reappeared with blue hair sprayed with gold and her face painted red and gold.

There is nothing so beautiful as two believers beginning their marriage in fellowship with God. Such marriages are quite rare in Muslim countries. Many a girl longs for a Christian husband but in despair gives in to marry whoever asks for her. Many Christian men face similar problems and need motherly suggestions as they try to find a mate. Early in my missionary work, I recognized that remaining single was not an easy option for Moroccans. I could see, too, that without Christian families, establishing a strong Moroccan church would be difficult. My matchmaking skills were sharpened as I counseled and prayed with young men and women over four decades. It seemed I was often a necessary key to success in their search for a believing mate. I pressed on to establish inter–mission and inter–city fellowships where a broad circle of friendships could develop.

I hope and pray that some Moroccan matchmaker has picked up where I left off.

Chapter 19

The Families Next Door

The local grocery shop, generally operated by a Soussi Berber from southern Morocco, is one of the most interesting stores in the marketplace. Soussis monopolize the merchandising in Morocco – grocery stores, dry goods, hardware stores and cloth markets. They are ambitious, honest, proud and intelligent. Soussi men often leave their wives in the hills of southern Morocco to farm their land while they go to distant cities to open businesses. Many sleep in their shops at night and keep their shops open sixteen hours a day, expertly blending into the commercial community while avoiding social contact with local people. At feast times they return to Soussi country to visit their wives and children.

When three Soussi brothers moved to Meknes, they broke tradition by bringing their wives and children with them. Each brother had about eight children, so the house they bought down the street from ours bulged with youngsters. The house had three stories, and each family claimed one floor. The men bought several shops in the town.

Soussi women, as we discovered, have their own culture. They dye their shiny dark hair black, and all of them, both young and old, wear bangs and have a long, shiny braid down their back. They embroider beautiful white scarves and always keep them draped over their heads. When any man, even a family member, passes by, they grab the scarves to cover their faces. Soussi women love to dance, joining arms and swaying back and forth, keeping the famous white scarves over their heads all the while. Their dance is not much more than the shuffling of feet, but their unique rhythmic chanting has etched itself permanently in my mind.

Getting to Know My Neighbors

When I met the Soussi family next door, one daughter had already married. One brother had moved his wife and children back to Soussi country to care for the land. He and one son remained with the families left in Meknes to operate their many shops. Eight girls from the two remaining families caused their cousin to call the home "a girls' sewing bee." The family that moved away had seven girls, and they sent one at a time to join the group in the city. Each was to adapt to city ways, learn the Arabic language and find a good Soussi husband with a prospering business.

The language of the home was Soussi, but all the girls attended an Islamic school where they studied in classical Arabic. They spoke the Moroccan dialect with difficulty. The older girls dropped out of school to help in the house when little ones were born. They did not mix with children in the street at play.

One Soussi mother worried because her girls didn't know how to knit, crochet or embroider. A friend told her the Americans next door taught girls these skills free of charge. Soussi always respond to the word "free." One day during our Vacation Bible School, three sisters from the Soussi house who had never been in my home before came over. These beautiful girls with their shiny black bangs and long braids chatted happily among themselves in the Soussi dialect. They considered themselves a superior race – to be born a Soussi was the most wonderful gift in the world. However, among our city girls they were very conspicuous.

How I loved the Soussi girls! A lovely, submissive, humble and intelligent girl, Nijma, soon enrolled in the classes. Her older sister, Malika, soon came to class as well, immediately getting into trouble with her teachers for her constant chatter. She couldn't imagine sitting that long without talking.

As the years went by, Naima, the oldest, came regularly and became interested in the gospel. She began studying a Navigators Bible study course in classical Arabic on her own and often came to our home to ask questions. She studied all the Navigators courses available, memorized Scripture, and one day came to tell us about her discovery of faith in Christ. Because she was the oldest girl in the family, she had many duties. Naima went to the market every day, made the beds for the whole family and cleaned all the floors. In spite of all she had to do, she hurried on Sundays and was always present for the fellowship meeting.

Naima loved to talk, too, and she became a good companion for my co-worker at the time, who also loved to talk. They continued to talk after Naima's mother called her home. They talked as they descended the long stairway, at the open doorway and at the end of the hallway. They talked in the *derb* long after many calls for her to come home. Much of their conversation had to do with the new life Naima had chosen. She grew quickly in faith and grace.

One of my expanding ministries after Sunset Farm closed down was Theological Education by Extension. In the mid-1970s I was preparing to hold a TEE class for some young men. Naima asked if she might join them. I wondered how she could attend classes with boys and how she would study her lessons. But Naima was intelligent, wise and ambitious. She pulled her lessons out at night and completed them by candlelight. She always attended the classes when they were in our home and often asked permission to attend the class when we held it in another city. A committee outside the country gave the final grades. Naima's grades far surpassed those of the four men in the class.

Naima put her knowledge to work, becoming a dependable Bible teacher. When she taught classes in our home, the young ladies sat up and took notice, realizing for the first time that this message was for them. Many girls became interested and some believed.

The Makings of a Christian Marriage

Since we no longer had access to Sunset Farm, we held a Bible conference in our home for young believers from various cities. Naima attended, meeting a young man from

Casablanca who was also a Soussi. He was so Soussi, in fact, that instead of being called by his name, Fuahd, people called him "Soussi." The two spent spare moments chatting in their mother tongue, getting acquainted.

Fuahd wanted Naima to write to him, but she was nervous about it. Her cousin had been seeing a young man at school whom she liked. When the family discovered the friendship, they quickly married her to a Soussi whom she had never seen. Nevertheless, Naima and Fuahd began to correspond. Fuahd sent all his letters to our house, where she picked them up.

Fuahd went to Lebanon to study at a Baptist seminary. They continued to write secretly until he returned in the summer to ask for her in marriage. He came to our home to plan with Naima how this should be done. They decided he would come with his uncle from Casablanca to her father's shop. He instructed his uncle not to tell Naima's father that they had met at my house or that they had been corresponding.

Fuahd and his uncle arrived during VBS while Naima was teaching a class. Fuahd came to our home and related what had happened at the shop. When Naima's father asked how they had met, Fuahd's uncle forgot all the careful instructions. He blurted out that they had met at my house and had been corresponding for a year.

"If he goes to the American's home he must be a good fellow," declared the father. He told Fuahd's uncle not to worry; he would talk it over with the women. Fuahd and his uncle went home with the father for dinner.

Naima was upset that things had not gone the way they had planned. She was sure that her father would refuse. Right there she decided she would never marry. Later she confessed to me that the Lord must love her a lot because He answered her prayer even though she hadn't believed.

The mother came to call on me that evening with a daughter to translate for her. She wanted to know about the young man's character, why he hadn't asked for her before he went to Lebanon and why they had been writing. Although Fuahd was a Soussi, he was not from the same tribe, which concerned her.

We assured her that all was well and that Fuahd was a good fellow. The father had given his word. To a Soussi, a man's word was as good as a contract.

You can imagine the excitement among the other girls in the Soussi household. "There comes Naima's man," they would whisper as they peeked around corners and from behind curtains. Fuahd always brought a bouquet of flowers when he called at the home, but he could never see Naima there. He saw her in secret at our house.

Naima's oldest brother called on me a few days after the engagement. He asked me if Naima truly wanted this engagement, because she was too embarrassed to talk to him about it. She wouldn't even respond. "We decided never to give our sisters to someone they didn't want," he said. Knowing Naima as well as I did, it was not at all difficult to assure him that this was what she wanted.

Naima's uncle was also a little nervous about the arrangement. He approached his brother with his concern: "This fellow may be a Christian. Did you ask him?"

"No," answered her father. "That is his business. Let him take care of himself." Sometime later her father met me on the street. Taking my hand, he said, "I have given Naima to Fuahd 'on your face' (because I have confidence in you). You are good people, and because he comes to you, he must be good, too." Such words were pleasant to hear, but it was startling to have to acknowledge the tremendous responsibility I had taken upon myself as a matchmaker.

Fuahd returned to seminary that fall, leaving his bride to plan the wedding for the following year. While he was gone, Naima asked to join two fellows who had announced their intention to be baptized. For years our baptisms had been at Sunset Farm, usually before a large audience at the baptismal pool. Memories of these baptisms crossed my mind briefly as we stood beside a bathtub to witness the baptism. It was a secret ceremony, and just as Naima entered the water her sisters called for her to come home. I made excuses, allowing her to stay long enough to complete the desire of her heart.

Watching Them Grow Up

All of the girls from the Soussi house came to classes at one time or another. In one VBS, Zuhura and Malika didn't behave well in class. Because of that, we didn't invite them to attend the "camp" we planned to have in our home later. We invited their sisters, Nijma and Azeeza, which hurt the pride of those left out. We never had difficulty with them again. Zuhura and Nijma became believers soon after the camp and became part of the fellowship.

Summer came and Fuahd arrived back from Lebanon for the wedding. Fuahd and his family had furnished a house in Casablanca for his bride. The night of the wedding, Fuahd's friends took Naima there.

Naima joined her husband in Lebanon, where she studied with him. They returned to Morocco fully equipped to carry on the Lord's work. They won other couples in Casablanca to Christ and frequently spent time in Soussi country witnessing to the grace of God. Fuahd prepared messages for radio broadcasts. He led the fellowship meetings in their city, and Naima taught the believing women.

Of all the Soussi girls, Nijma was my special crown and joy. If I needed help with cleaning the house or cooking a meal, an extra teacher or a prayer partner, she was always there. When I wanted to give a lesson on *Pilgrim's Progress* to a class and had only the text in classical Arabic, I gave it to Nijma, who then presented it to the class in Moroccan Arabic.

It was a big disappointment to me when I learned of Nijma's engagement to an unbeliever. Nijma did not want this marriage. Her father insisted on it because the man was a relative and wealthy. "I am older than you, and I know what is best for you," he explained to his daughter.

Nijma's fiance came to see me later, complaining that the girl did not want him. He couldn't understand why she would not see him or talk to him. He asked me to try to find out the reason. Of course I knew the answer. Nijma did not want the marriage and had never consented to it. Since her father was standing nearby when the *cadi* came, she had not replied to his question. As had happened with other girls, they took her silence for consent.

Nijma's aunt described the wedding as more like a funeral. The bride cried for two days before the ceremony. I attended the elaborate affair at her home. When she had dressed and had gone to the car to be driven to Marrakech with members of her family, she wept bitterly. Although I was invited to go along, I chose not to attend the remainder of the wedding. Nijma now lives in Marrakech and works as a lawyer. She has three children.

With the help of Fuahd, I arranged the marriage of Zuhura to a Berber who was not a Soussi. Perhaps Nijma's tears had softened the hearts of family members, who accepted Fuahd's choice for a husband "on his face."

Four of the remaining Soussi girls were believers. I loved them all dearly, and if these, my neighbors, had been the only fruit of my labors I would have considered my ministry blessed indeed.

Chapter 20

More Room in My Heart

As you can see, just one household on my block filled many hours and covered many years with involvement enough to keep me occupied. Hundreds more in my "parish" also looked to me for encouragement from day to day. I knew Hania, Kinza, Malika and Rachida as little girls, saw them grow up to profess Christ and be baptized, and struggled with them through their engagements and marriages to unbelievers. I shared their sorrow when they could no longer attend meetings and more than once planned a meeting to get them together. I also invited several other young women to these meetings. Because these women could not get out easily, the best encouragement I could give them was to go to their homes, one at a time.

A sensitive girl, Zuhoor's tears fell easily whenever she related her many trials. She lived in a neighborhood considered "holy" since only descendants of the prophet Muhammad could live there. Her parents had emigrated from a holy city 200 miles east across the mountains, a city where many Arabs first settled when they came to Morocco. From that city came the ancestors of the Sultan. As a bride, Zuhoor's mother rode a donkey across those 200 miles.

Zuhoor was about eight years old when her friends brought her to my classes. She was a good student and memorized many Bible verses, earning her a place in Bible camp. When she heard the gospel for the first time, she readily accepted the fact of Jesus' death, although the teaching opposes Islamic belief. Zuhoor wanted to bring her friends to me so they could hear and understand the gospel. She also earned a Bible, and when she took it home, her parents did not object.

According to her birth certificate, Zuhoor was only fourteen when someone asked for her in marriage. Her parents had her birth date changed legally, a small matter.

Having never seen this man, Zuhoor was inquisitive. She wanted to know what he was like, so her sister helped her arrange to meet him. They met in the shadows of a dark street corner to get acquainted.

When her parents discovered this shameful act, they were furious. They soon broke off the engagement. I was delighted with this news, but my joy didn't last long. When other parents came to ask for her, she was engaged again and soon gone.

Shortly after Zuhoor had moved into her husband's home, her mother–in–law came with her to a meeting I had arranged for the young women who had married unbelievers. Her presence made ministry to Zuhoor difficult. As I learned later, the mother–in–law was cruel and selfish, doting on her two grown sons and making life miserable for Zuhoor.

Zuhoor's husband was free to go wherever he wished. He attended parties and places of entertainment regularly while she stayed home and took care of her babies. He drank heavily and had mistresses. When one mistress became pregnant, he promised to marry the girl, divorce her after the child was born and take Zuhoor and her children to France. It was a wild promise. He never divorced the second wife; she had more children. He did move Zuhoor out of his parents' home into a house of her own, but soon the new wife also moved into the house. Zuhoor could not live with the second wife. She took her children and moved back with her in–laws.

After being absent from the meetings for a long time, Zuhoor attended a conference. I shall never forget her words, which pierced all of our hearts. She stood up and, after thanking the Lord for the privilege of meeting again with believers, asked, "How many of you have been praying for me while I have been absent?"

Silence hung over the room for a few moments, and I realized how faithless I had been in my prayers.

Zuhoor moved out of the in–laws' home to a room of her own. Her husband never supported her or her children. One day as he was leaving for a month's vacation he stopped by.

He seemed very sympathetic over her financial situation and left her the equivalent of eighty-five cents.

The strain of trying to support three children became too much for Zuhoor. She began to have fainting spells and cried constantly. All this time she remained faithful to her husband. She trusted him completely as he made promise after promise that he never kept. I pleaded with her not to trust him any longer, but to trust the Lord to care for her and her children.

We were preparing a Christmas party and invited Zuhoor. While waiting for the party to start, she took the children to the public bath where they could keep warm on that cold day. At noon she spent her few coins on bread for the children. By the time they arrived at our home for the party she was so weak that she fell. We offered milk to both her and the children, but she refused her share, urging us to give it to the children.

Zuhoor moved in with us and applied for a divorce, hoping to get more money for the children's support. The paperwork was staggering. One day we thought she was dying when she fainted and we could feel no pulse. When she revived, she asked me to call her husband, which I did. He promised to come immediately, but he never came. Later we heard that he had hoped she would die and relieve him of the responsibility.

With help from her brothers, Zuhoor got the divorce. Even then she got no money; her ex-husband found a way to divert the funds to his second wife. It took many trips to the capital city to finally settle the matter, transferring the funds to Zuhoor. This left her indignant ex-husband angry enough to move away to hide from the government and from Zuhoor.

Zuhoor found work as a teacher's aid in a preschool. She went early to ride the bus to pick up the children and remained with the bus until they had taken every child home. The days were long and the pay was small, but her love for children kept her there. Arab women are very proud. Zuhoor was determined to provide at least a meager living for her own children.

Zuhoor loved her children dearly. Her family wanted her to give the children to their father and force him to provide for them, allowing her to remarry. Refusing to turn her children over to the other wife, she found a better job in the courthouse. She struggled financially, borrowing money to keep her children clothed and in school. Budgeting was not a Moroccan custom and she turned down my efforts to help her learn this foreign skill.

I had just returned to Morocco from a short furlough in the States when Zuhoor came to see me. Imagine my surprise to learn that she had taken her worthless husband back! In tears, she told me about the big mistake she had made. She did it because the children begged her to. They wanted him to come home now and then so they could see him. At first he helped a little, but not for long. His second wife was furious when she discovered the remarriage, and that ended that.

Did this story end well? I think so. God can turn all things to good in the lives of believers. Zuhoor seldom came to Fellowship meetings; like many working mothers here in the United States, she complained that on Sundays she had to do the family laundry, shop and visit the sick and mourning.

Since the oldest boy, Abd Allah, spent his first ten years with his grandparents, he was a devout Muslim when he came to live with his mother. But when someone stole his shoes while he prayed at the mosque, he lost faith in Islam. After he accepted the death and sonship of Christ, he wanted to share his joy with everyone. He asked American tourists he met strolling the streets of Meknes if they loved Jesus.

Abd Allah was sharp in school and often confronted his teachers with the truth. He met some important leaders from the mosque and began discussions with them. He became a speaker at our Sunday Fellowship, and the group preferred him above everyone else.

The two younger children filled their mother's place in the Fellowship. The little ones had attended classes from an early age, and they had their mother for spiritual encouragement. They found it easy to believe. The children returned the love and compassion their mother gave them. She still lived in tears, but she found a reward in the affection of her children and the knowledge they had all come to know Christ.

Fruits of Early Labors

While Zuhoor's children became solid members of the Christian fellowship, I knew grandchildren of early Christians who also grew into faithful believers in Christ. A woman named Fatima had accepted Christ during the early ministry of Maude Cary. She lived in a section of Meknes called Dar Elkibira. A big sign over the entry gate read, "All foreigners are forbidden to enter." I was a new missionary when Miss Cary first took me to Dar Elkibira, and I was surprised that we ignored the sign and walked right in.

The main street through this part of town was probably about ten feet in width. Fifty-foot high crumbling walls towered above both sides of the street, which was covered with a dome roof. Swallows made their nests in the crevices of these old walls. The area was dark, musty and spooky. We stumbled around potholes in the dirt streets, with hardly enough light to see them. We passed at least one water fountain tucked away in a corner surrounded by dozens of carriers who had come to get water for use in their households. Animal and human dung lay along the sides of the streets. Our voices echoed as we traveled this winding path. Occasionally we passed alleys that led to places of habitation. Children, hearing our voices, dashed out of the alleys looking for ways to entertain themselves.

The district had been built for the children born to the concubines of King Ishmael, who in the seventeenth century had made Meknes the imperial city. While legally he could have only four wives, he had many concubines. Today the district is considered holy, and only descendants of the apostle Muhammad can live there.

As the years went by, we often called at the home of Hassan, who lived in this ancient rubble. His grandmother came to weekly meetings in our home. His mother always welcomed us, and his grandmother loved to show off her grandchildren. The family lived in one room where they cooked, ate and slept. Sitting in the room, we looked out the door and saw only walls.

Hassan was ambitious, studying hard and dreaming of the day when he could find a more suitable place for his family to live. He brought Sidi Mustapha to class, a friend who also lived among the high walls. Sidi Mustapha, who rarely ventured much farther than Dar Elkibira and the spice shop his father operated, was amazed when he entered our home. Here were two foreign women dressed in Moroccan clothes and speaking the Moroccan dialect of Arabic. When he came to us, he had never heard of missionaries or the gospel.

We studied the gospel of Luke with a few other boys at a weekly class, but Sidi Mustapha was so fascinated he would come during the week also. He was a well-disciplined lad, obedient to his parents and respectful of others. He had attended government camps, which offered an opportunity to leave the dark alleys of home and enjoy sunshine and open spaces, so he eagerly accepted our invitation to Bible camp. Following camp, one of my co-workers began a Bible study class for Sidi Mustapha and four of his friends. On their way home from that class, they would stop at my home to ask questions: "How can Jesus be God?" "What will happen to us when we die?"

I was sure that Sidi Mustapha was a believer long before he confessed it. Although he prayed with us and participated in all our activities, he would never say he believed. When a guest from London asked him if he was a believer, he finally admitted it. This confession made a big difference in his life.

Hassan dropped out of classes when he entered the university. Later he became a judge at the city court, and his dream of moving his family to better living conditions came true. Sidi Mustapha, who didn't like to study, taught Arabic at a Christian orphanage in another town, where his quiet, friendly personality served him well. He joined the Theological Education by Extension studies in the 1970s. We often met at the orphanage for our classes. During that period he was baptized at Derb Skat in a service with two other believers.

When I had to return to the United States for health reasons, I left Sidi Mustapha in charge of the house. Each Sunday he opened the doors for the fellowship meetings and carried on all year, mending quarrels and keeping the group together. Before I returned to Morocco, Sidi Mustapha visited Kansas City, where I introduced him to the staff at Gospel Missionary Union's International Headquarters. While he was in Kansas City, he gave his testimony to the mission's board members. When he saw a familiar face in the group, a former worker in Morocco, he gave him the usual Moroccan greeting. To avoid offending the other members of the board, he made the rounds, kissing each board member on both cheeks in the same manner. They were shocked, but they loved him for it.

Year after year, Sidi Mustapha tried to pass the baccalaureate, the difficult examination required to receive his high–school diploma. When at last he received it, he took teacher's training and became a school teacher. He was sent to a primitive place across the Atlas Mountains. When students in this school were too poor to buy the books required, he provided them. He often bought clothes or shoes for those who suffered from the cold.

This young man taught me some classical Arabic, the customs of the land, Moroccan manners and a great deal about Moroccan cooking. He instructed me on the art of speaking politely without telling everything I knew and how to know when to be quiet. He seemed to have a special gift of discernment and could tell if people were sincere or not.

Sidi Mustapha's dream of attending Bible college in the United States was never realized, but he loved to study the Word of God. He rejoiced in the fact that he had eternal life and no longer feared death. His favorite book of the Bible was Hebrews because it emphasized the importance of the blood of Christ and His death. His favorite verses were Romans 8:31–32, "If God is for us, who can be against us? He who did not spare his own Son, but gave him up for us all – how will he not also, along with him, graciously give us all things?"

I have many sons and daughters in the faith who are very special to me, but Sidi Mustapha has been extra-special. I think of the words of our Lord Jesus, who said, "No one who has left home or wife or brothers or parents or children for the sake of the kingdom of God will fail to receive many times as much in this age and, in the age to come, eternal life" (Luke 18:29–30). Though we are now miles and cultures apart, I rejoice that we had such fellowship.

Chapter 21

The Valley of the Shadow

Of all the Soussi girls, Malika was the most faithful Christian. She had a grasp of truth beyond her years, and nothing could deter her from her desire to live solely for Christ.

Malika allowed herself to become a slave to the entire Soussi household, to the point of being denied an education because she was needed at home. Despite a heavy load of responsibility, she always arrived first for a meeting. She insisted that her sister Mikilsoum enroll in the university and picked up her share of the work at home to make it possible.

Malika wanted to marry a believer, but her parents finally gave her to a Muslim, a Soussi who lived in Meknes. Her health began to deteriorate after the engagement, but she refused to see a doctor. When she had no more strength left, her family sought medical help, only to discover she had cancer. The family refused to accept this diagnosis. They tried every cure of their own, every method they could think of to build up her strength before the wedding.

Finally they allowed me to take Malika to a specialist in another city. He insisted on hospitalizing her; the family reluctantly allowed her to be admitted. She took with her to the hospital the words of Psalm 23: "Though I walk through the valley of the shadow of death, I will fear no evil, for you are with me." And in that hospital, Malika died.

Seeing Death Through Their Eyes

Millions of people spend dismal and lonely last hours facing death without knowing the blessed truth Malika embraced. In many Christless societies, when a person dies, an agonizing cry fills the air, symbolizing the widespread hopelessness in the face of death and the dreadful fear of the unknown. When Paul wrote, "We do not want you to . . . grieve like the rest of men, who have no hope" (1 Thessalonians 4:13), he explained that death for the believer is simply "falling asleep" in Christ, only to awaken in heaven and be with the Lord forever. Believers also feel sorrow – we mourn the loss of the companionship and the physical presence of our loved ones. There is no need, however, for our death wails to resound relentlessly as if there were no hope. We weep for ourselves, not for the one who has gone to be with Christ.

In Morocco, death wails and moans during the night often awakened me. Mourning women gouged their beautiful faces with their fingernails until the blood ran down their cheeks.

Burial in Morocco takes place very soon after death. When daylight comes and the stores open, the men buy several yards of white linen in which to wrap the deceased. They also buy meat to feed funeral guests. The mourners who come to pay their respects soon fill the house.

The mosque teacher washes the body according to the same legal rites of purification every Muslim goes through before he prays. After the ceremonial washing, the body is saturated with fragrant perfumes and wrapped in a linen shroud. There is no embalming in Morocco. If the deceased is a man, the family wraps the body in a palmetto mat. Women and little children are often buried in caskets. Even in death, a woman is not to be seen by men.

Carriers of the dead soon arrive with a bier and place the body on it. They hoist the bier onto their shoulders and as they head out the door, the male mourners follow, chanting parts of the Qur'an along the way. As the carriers take the body out of the house, a member of the family places a bowl of flour at the door. Each person in the procession takes a pinch, raises it in the air and says, "May God welcome him and make him happy." The leftover flour is given to the poor as alms.

Before the next prayer call if possible, the body is placed in a shallow grave facing Mecca, as if in prayer. The mourners return to the home for a brief, agonizing time of mourning, then partake of the funeral feast.

The second day, women go to the grave carrying spices and perfumes to sprinkle around the fresh mound. Their faces are badly scarred from mourning the previous day. On the third day, hundreds of poor sit along the street near the home of the deceased, expecting the family to serve them a dish of couscous. They eat in the street, as many as ten men gathered around one tray of couscous.

Grieving men let their beards grow for forty days as a sign of mourning, and the women wear white clothing and use no cosmetics. Out of respect for the dead, the relatives visit the tomb at least once or twice a year. One custom is to sprinkle the grave with water. Muslims believe sprinkling abandoned graves brings merit in heaven.

City cemeteries are quiet places. The early missionaries cautioned the new language students not to spend time in or around them. Moroccans believe that after the soul leaves the body, it hovers around the house for three days and around the tomb for forty more days. After that, it returns to earth each Friday to visit the tomb. The reality of evil spirits in third-world countries is evident to missionaries, and as language students, we heeded our seniors' advice.

Finding Jewels in the Hardest Places

Pioneer missionaries worked for years seeing no converts and for decades seeing very few. Many believe that in the early days, families dealt with those who converted to Christianity by poisoning them. Promising inquirers often became ill and died in those days, no questions asked.

Without a doubt, though, there were secret conversions in the early days. Haddou might have been one of them.

We knew Haddou as an old man. This charming patriarch came from the mountains above Sefrou where the winters are cold and even summer mornings are nippy, so he wore home-woven woolen garments. His outer garment was a *jelaba* with a hood that covered his white turban. A thick white beard, neatly trimmed, covered the lower portion of his face, leaving only his nose and piercing brown eyes exposed to the elements.

We loved the old man, who eventually came to our Bible conferences at Sunset Farm. His story thrilled us all. When Haddou was just a boy, pioneer missionary Victor Swanson had become acquainted with his father, the chief of a Berber village, at the Sefrou market and had gained *mizrug-allah* – the promise of protection – from him. Swanson moved into Haddou's home, where night after night he preached the gospel to anyone who came in. In his heart, Haddou believed the good things he was hearing. Then Swanson left the village, and for a long time, perhaps fifty years, Haddou never heard the gospel again.

Life in the country became hard for Haddou, and the walk to the Sefrou market was too long. In his old age he bought a piece of ground outside the city and built a room where he lived with his family.

Haddou's grandson married a girl who had attended the girls' class at the Sefrou mission house. One day she invited Signe Johnson to come to her home. Haddou was overjoyed to hear the gospel again, and he recounted his story to Miss Johnson. For about four years, he attended meetings or dropped in for coffee and the reading of the Word. When a missionary visited his humble home, his first question would be, "Where is the Book? Bring it out and read it to me!"

Haddou had never been baptized, so we discussed the matter with him at a Bible conference where we planned to have a baptismal service. This old gentleman had probably had his last bath in a river as a young man. His heart was solely Christ's, but the idea of being dipped under water on a cold spring day was totally foreign to him. After thinking it over, however, he decided that at the next conference he would be baptized.

The conference was scheduled for April. In March, however, the Lord took Haddou home. As he lay dying on a Sunday afternoon, Signe Johnson paid a visit to his home. Even in his weakened state, he recognized her and seemed happy she had come. She entered the room, where his friends and relatives surrounded him. His brother had brought a Muslim reader, who took his place beside the bed and began to recite a chapter from the Qur'an. The selected portion mentioned the lot of "blasphemers," and Signe supposed the passage was directed to her. When he finished his chapter, he raised his finger above Haddou and witnessed to Muhammad. The dying man looked troubled, but he was helpless to defend himself.

When the reader left, Signe stepped up to the bed and began to recite Scripture. She spoke about God's love in sending a Savior who paid for our sins. She reminded Haddou and other believing members of his family that Christ had ascended into heaven to prepare a place for all who place their trust in Him. After speaking a little while, she told Haddou that she had to leave him but that the Lord was by his side. A smile spread over Haddou's face.

Haddou's family buried him the next morning in the traditional manner. Only later did his wife advise Signe that he was gone.

Death strikes the old, the young, the rich, the poor. It has no favorites. I have met wrinkled old men and women who boasted that they were 120 years old – old enough, as they say, to have grown a third set of teeth! They, too, finally found their resting places in shallow graves. Many were too poor to afford grave markers, and their graves were so shallow that dogs dug up the unknown bodies.

A young friend who just days before had taken me to the doctor died when his car rolled down a ravine. A young teacher who had often been in our home was driving home from school when her car skidded into a cistern and she drowned. A child was struck by a car and died. Babies died because they had a bad case of diarrhea and were taken to the doctor too late. I have consoled widows of the king's ministers whose husbands were executed after an attempted coup. Again and again, I have witnessed the truth of Psalm 89:48,

"What man can live and not see death, or save himself from the power of the grave?"

Today, Muslims make up about one-fifth of the world's population. The Muslim community in England is mushrooming. Mosques are proliferating in France, and Arab leaders boldly predict that Islam will take over America in a few years.

These startling facts awaken us to the need to pray as we have never prayed before for Muslims, for missionaries to Muslims, for international students and for converts from Islam. Prayer is effective. God changed His mind about destroying His disobedient children when Moses prayed earnestly (Exodus 32:10–14). Let us believe in the power of prayer for Islam today. Many are dying each day with no hope.

We also need to take a good look at the zeal of Muslims who are seeking converts from western countries. Our interest lags by comparison.

While the Muslim world is considered among the most difficult to reach for Christ, we must continue to go to Muslims. As in the process of searching for rare jewels, God's finest rewards await those who search in the hardest of places. One believer dying peacefully in the knowledge that the sacrificial Christ has paid the price for his sins – one dear saint like Haddou – or one convert living victoriously in the strength of Christ more than makes up for any trials and tears encountered along the way.

Chapter 22

Building a Fellowship That Will Last

One busy Saturday morning long ago, the Peabody family, with whom I shared a telephone in Khemisset, got a call from Wilma Friesen at Sunset Farm. A little girl had been born prematurely to the wife of a new Christian, Moulay Idriss. Since I had often visited their home, they asked if I would come to help. The baby was still alive, but she appeared to have little hope of survival in the primitive setting in which she had been born. Since Edithmae Peabody was a nurse, I asked her to go along.

We stooped to enter the dark hut and found the mother, Humoosha, on a raised bed that occupied half the hut. Neighboring women and children filled the rest of the room. We asked to see the little one, and when Edithmae unwrapped the bundle, she expressed amazement that such a tiny infant could have survived eight hours since her birth. Three months premature, the tiny baby had hair growing across her forehead down to her eyelashes.

We both prayed silently, not sure what we should do. The baby did not have much chance to survive, so we hesitated to accept the responsibility of taking her. We did not want the family to blame us for the baby's death. On the other hand, the infant obviously needed twenty-four-hour care that she wouldn't receive in the hut. Later in the day, Moulay Idriss settled the matter by giving permission for Humoosha and the baby to come and stay with me.

We estimated the weight of the baby to be about two pounds. We fed her every two hours with a medicine dropper. Getting the milk down was a tedious task, and by the time we finished one feeding, it was almost time for the next. From the beginning, the strength of that little body amazed us. In a cardboard box heated by two hot-water bottles, she continued to gain strength and battle for her life. Meanwhile, Humoosha was getting a good dose of spiritual food as she listened to us read and explain portions from the Word of God. One morning I had the joy of leading Humoosha to accept the Lord Jesus as her Savior.

After two weeks, Humoosha went home, and we were left with the full care of the baby. Edithmae, with a large family of her own, offered to take her. In that home full of loving care and plenty of babysitters, the Berber baby thrived. The parents named her Lila Saadia and dedicated her to the Lord. But each time they took her home, she became sick, and back to Edithmae she went. Lila Saadia lived and became a beautiful child, although she had malformed legs.

Building a fellowship in a Muslim country resembles parenting a family. Some converts we might least expect to thrive, like Lila Saadia, become strong and spread joy. Yet even with the best of parenting, some die; some are weak; some stumble easily; some are led astray.

When the government cracked down on foreign missionaries, the Lord moved my colleagues to a broadened range of ministries outside Morocco. However, I believed He had brought me back to Meknes so I could continue to train Moroccan believers to carry on the ministry, with or without a missionary present. I was aware of the many potential problems – we had been praying, planning and working toward building a Moroccan church for nearly twenty years.

Helping the Church Mature

Sunday services and general conferences had been held in Derb Skat before I arrived in Morocco. During the services, the men sat on benches on one end of the room, and women sat on mats placed on the floor on the other end. In the early days Berber men from Mijjot walked in from the country to attend. They were faithful to the Lord, coming in secret when times were hard to hear the Word of God.

Missionaries had primarily conducted the meetings. We attempted to involve the Moroccans in service and learned many lessons through our experience. We gave two young fellows the job of taking up the offering. In their eyes, the small offerings were large. The two young men grew covetous and began to contemplate ways to benefit from the money themselves. We learned our first lesson: don't put temptation before the eyes of new believers.

One participant was a good student and an excellent reader. Since he had a talent for public speaking, he gave messages occasionally, but he was spiritually immature. We learned to heed the Scriptural advice about novices and to give new converts time to mature (1 Timothy 3:6).

We expatriates handled all the rules and regulations. We set the time of the meetings, decided what room we would meet in, led the meetings and made all other decisions. But we weren't merely entertaining guests in our home; we were dealing with potential church members. Since it was to be their church, we needed to teach decision-making by sharing the responsibility of making decisions.

Our next lesson came to us in a much more startling and forceful manner. We had no restrictions on who could come to the meetings. A young teacher from another town had been held in jail for several months because of radical political literature found in his apartment. Immediately upon his release from jail, he made his way to our home and attended a believers meeting. This caused our own people to shudder with fear because we always tried to avoid politics.

The teacher began to bring others to our meetings, some of them attracted by the fact that women were present. The women became uncomfortable because these fellows didn't show the common courtesy they were accustomed to receiving from the local believers. We heard that one young man was a great believer and that he brought friends to his apartment to hear the Word of God. We lent him some tapes and books, which he never returned. One of our men found the tapes for sale on the street. He bought them and brought them back to us to prove the fraudulent claims of this group.

Becoming Self-Sufficient

It had always been our hope, prayer and goal to let go of the reins and allow the Moroccans to take control. The time finally came. I had begun to teach the TEE (Theological Education by Extension) program to five students, which gave me an excellent opportunity to put their knowledge to work. This was the fruition of years of laying a foundation, a time of transferring the leadership of the church to the Moroccans. The transition came naturally because I, a woman and now their sole teacher, was on my own. Many of them had known me since their childhood and knew me too well to feel threatened or hindered by my presence. The fact that the American "brothers" were gone made a natural bridge for the Moroccan believers to reach out to help me.

As a group, the Moroccan church made its own rules, chose its own elders, named the fellowship and gave each member some responsibility. It appointed some to visit the sick, some to visit those who missed meetings and some to provide refreshments to serve after the meetings.

Ideally located, Derb Skat offered both space and privacy, so no one raised a question about where the fellowship might meet. The group decided no one should attend the meetings unless the chosen elders approved. This lifted a big load off my shoulders because they knew their own people far better than I did. They also decided that each member of the group should give some money each month according to his ability. Two Southern Baptist workers from the Near East once held a seminar in our home for the believers. When the workers finished the course, the elders from the fellowship handed them money for their services. Astonished but pleased with this gesture, the guests thanked the believers heartily.

The fellowship members chose the room they wanted to meet in and, using fellowship money, furnished it with a rug, mattresses and covers for the couches, a center table and curtains for the windows. They preferred to sit in a circle, since sitting in rows is impolite in their culture.

Five of the believers took turns each Sunday speaking and leading worship. If one couldn't come when it was his turn, I filled in. I always found it necessary to have sermons prepared because I sometimes had to speak on short notice. The fellowship grew in strength and influence. Those who were available met each week for prayer.

The group served communion once a month. We canned grape juice, which we served from a large common glass, and cut up ordinary bread. Limited to baptized believers, communion was a special time none of them wanted to miss. Baptism demanded a difficult and costly break with Islam, a valid recognition of the believer's sincerity.

The idea of attending meetings regularly each week was new to the fellowship group, so I had to teach them this idea. Some took the advice seriously and put aside every duty to be present. They felt it wasn't fair for the speaker to work so hard in preparation and not have an audience. Some worked all week and used Sundays for laundry; others had exams to study for; still others had company drop in, and custom didn't allow them to leave; or others met friends on their way to fellowship and went with them instead. When they came to me later in the day expecting me to give them the message they missed, I gladly did so; but I told them that hearing about the morning message is like eating warmed–over couscous.

We normally met on Sunday, but during Ramadan, which was always a problem for Moroccan believers, we met on Saturday night. If they met at night, no one could accuse them of eating at the mission house during the day. Thus, we often held meetings during Ramadan at about midnight, after the family meals that followed the prayer call at sundown.

Learning Through Challenges

Moroccans do not observe the Christmas holiday, but the fellowship enjoyed setting aside a day near December 25 to celebrate the birth of Christ. It could not always be on Christmas Day because business and government offices were open. I tried to think of new ways to observe Christmas that would make it a special day for those who attended.

Each Christmas a teacher of higher education called on me. I had previously given him some Bible study, but I didn't trust him enough to invite him to the fellowship. One Christmas he came with his wife, and I felt it necessary to entertain him properly. I invited the couple to the upper floor living quarters, ushered them into the living room and then went to the kitchen for coffee.

In the room was a box of books a friend had brought me the week before. There were books written by a former missionary in Algeria and translated into French, as well as other literature. When I returned with the coffee, the teacher asked me for a book. Not trusting him, I turned him down, but I handed him a calendar from the box. On the front were the words "God Is Love," and in small letters was the reference 1 John 4:16.

The next day as we prepared for the Christmas party, a policeman came to the door. He pulled a card from his pocket and asked if I had given it to anyone. Recognizing the calendar, I thought of the teacher. I admitted that I had, and he asked me to bring out any literature I had in the house. I brought him the box of books, which he took to the police station. He asked me to meet him there, and he added with a sneer: "Would you give poison to anyone who asked for it?" I explained that what I had to offer people was not poison. Everyone should know about God's love.

At the police station I was questioned thoroughly. They let me go, but told me the books would have to stay until they had time to read them and study the contents. When I returned at the specified time, the officer informed me that the books were good. He turned to his colleague and told him how much he liked the explanation that man is separated from God and that Jesus has showed us how to approach God again. After this delightful comment, he turned to me and told me I could give the books to anyone I wanted, but I couldn't sell them.

Some time later, I was walking in the street near my home when from behind me I heard someone say, "God is love." I turned around to see who had spoken. It was the policeman who had come to the house with the calendar.

The church's transition to Moroccan leadership covered all areas. The maturing of Christians I had known from childhood and my own aging made the passing along of responsibilities a natural process. When I was ready to give up such joys as planning believers' weddings and catering for the receptions, they were prepared to act as hosts. Members of the fellowship group excelled in organizing, preparing food and welcoming the guests. One groom remarked that he didn't have to prepare a thing because the fellowship members had done everything ahead of time.

Sadly, divorces were common in the fellowship group. In Morocco we have never seen divorce occur when both husband and wife are believers. They take the Bible literally and believe God is not pleased with anyone breaking the marriage vow. But many young Christian women and some young men are married to unbelievers against their will. After a divorce, they came back to meetings, free to worship with us again. Many young women in our fellowship were divorced.

Hamid, a tall, fair, prosperous businessman, married. His mother wasn't pleased with his bride, so she sent her away. Hamid decided he wanted to marry a believer the next time. He couldn't find one he wanted to marry, so he married a Muslim girl, hoping that he might win her to Christ.

He asked for baptism and a date was set. His wife did attend meetings, but instead of accepting the love of the believers, she found things to criticize. Things became so confused that the baptism was canceled and never again arranged for Hamid. He asked me not to return to his home to continue Bible study with his wife because she was angry with me for defending the believers. It was a clear case when the enemy "sowed tares among the wheat" (Matthew 13:25 NKJV). Today Hamid comes to fellowship meetings without his wife's knowledge.

To make matters worse, Hamid made the pilgrimage to Mecca. He explained that he was going to accompany a female relative who would pay all the expenses. This gave him the title *hajji*, which I and a few members of the group refused to use. The elders discussed the danger of accepting him back but later decided that more harm might be done to the fellowship by turning him down.

Such decisions were struggles of immense proportions, even for the Moroccans. How much better equipped they were to make them than I!

Chapter 23

Jesus Led Me All the Way

The early 1970s passed quickly. Various Christian groups and summer missionaries visited me to help with the ministry. Perhaps even more important, Moroccans I had trained over many years, both men and women, proved to be capable teachers ready to lift the load. This was a great blessing when, early in 1978, I was first hospitalized in Morocco and then cared for by my colleagues across the Mediterranean in Spain. I had an infection around the lining of my heart and had to limit my activities – no long walks, stairs or housework. Since my house had many stairs, I found my illness frustrating.

I arrived back in Meknes in May, at the beginning of summer activities. Four students from Moody Bible Institute helped me prepare various meetings, a retreat for young ladies and a boys' retreat. After the Moody students left, our older Moroccan girls conducted a retreat for teenage girls. A Campus Crusade group came later that summer, and on the last afternoon of their meetings, two Christians were married at Derb Skat.

My illness culminated in a visit to the United States, where a heart specialist found that I had an invalid cardiac infarction – heart failure. Part of the heart muscle had been damaged and could not be repaired. What an inner struggle I went through! The doctor said he could not give consent to my return to Morocco, not even to gather up my belongings. Emotionally upset, I didn't want to see or talk to anyone. I kept asking God, "Why? How can it be?"

But the Lord knew what He was doing. I left for a missionary conference in Florida. The messages were just what I needed to hear. I came back to the mission headquarters in Kansas City in better condition and able to think more clearly. Greatest of all, I was open to God's precious will. The specialist was happy with the improvement and amazed at the strength I had. He consented to a short trip to Morocco. Mission officials decided to give me a three-month trial period, and I was soon on my way home.

My aim in returning was to help the fellowship group get better organized and prepare a program aimed at entire independence. I advised and challenged them. They assumed responsibility for most of the work, taking the burden from me. Each believer began seeing the need to reach out to others, to help with financial burdens and the spiritual ministry. Problems still existed, but the believers began to develop a greater sense of responsibility to each other and less dependence on the missionary. Shortly after I returned, the fellowship held a special course to prepare eight or nine believers for baptism, with a baptismal service at the end of the course. The fellowship prepared its constitution in writing and its schedule for the coming year.

My three-month trial period passed. Thanks to the strength the Lord gave me and capable help from the Moroccan Christians, I stayed on. A young co-worker, Larry McFall, arrived in September 1982 after having received his master's degree in Teaching English as a Second Language (TESL) – something that legitimized his presence in the country since no one could enter with a missionary visa. He was a great companion with good ideas, energy, zeal and determination to learn the language. His main goal was to train our men to lead and disciple others. Four neighborhood men who had grown up in my classes took a new interest; all were professionals, except one who was nearly finished with his studies at the university. I felt a new dimension of enthusiasm return to Derb Skat.

Two years later, after a brief furlough in the United States, my co-worker brought his bride, Sue, to Morocco to help in the work. Excitedly I prepared the house for her.

Tensions Rise

In 1984 the government began to probe the activities of believers throughout the country. Police sought out believers, examined them and cast them in jail. As word came to us, we knew that Meknes would not be spared. The government brought in one member of the fellowship, Abdullah, who went to his brother on the police force. He soon realized that this was not a local affair but a national one. The king had been rebuked for tolerating Christian activities in the land, so he had begun to take action. The police released Abdullah, but they watched him closely.

Abdullah knew they would soon target him, and they did. Government officials confiscated his literature and threw him in jail – a large room in the basement of the police station, already filled with criminals of every description. He sat and slept on the cement floor without so much as a mat. His mother brought him food each day. The fellowship suggested we not call on him because it would only cause him more trouble.

After several weeks, all our people were set free – all, that is, except Abdullah. Had he been forgotten? Some from our fellowship visited his mother from time to time and brought us news. We sent things by way of his mother to let the young man know we had not forgotten him and were praying for him.

After three months, his mother began to fear they would soon kill him. We had to do something. I knew that Allal, a wealthy businessman who operated a shop near our home, was a friend of the chief of police. Prayerfully I called on him at his shop and told him our problem, explaining that the authorities had forgotten Abdullah. He promised he would see what could be done, and the next day Abdullah came to our door. He was free at last, but he could hardly walk because he had sat on the cement floor of the prison for so long. Since he already had a passport, he arranged to leave the country as soon as he felt it was safe to do so.

Meanwhile, we had callers from the police department. They were suspicious because a couple was living with me at the time. They asked about several individuals, including Aisha, although they did not know her last name. I had an idea whom they meant, but I told them I needed the last name because Aisha is a common name.

The same was true for Rachida, although I knew of whom they spoke. They also asked for several men. Although they had last names for these men, I didn't know them, so I gave the police a negative response. After one of the men had looked around through the rooms of the house, they left.

I quickly ran to Aisha's home to tell her not to come. She came anyway, wanting more information about what was going on. We saw several men posted at the end of the alley and on the street, but with three other homes in our alley, it was never clear to which house people were going. Only once did they stop and question anyone, and that was a woman and her daughter.

A few days later another officer came to the door. This time they wanted me. I went with the officer to the police car parked out on the main road. As I chatted casually with the officer, I thought about the Moroccan believers who had gone through the same trauma. The courtesy the police showed me as an American woman was an exception to the rule.

I was ushered before the Chief of Police, who questioned me: "How did you enter Morocco in the first place?"

"I came as a missionary with a French visa."

"Do you still carry on this work? I mean, do people still come to you?"

I was registered now as a teacher, but I replied truthfully: "Of course they do. They are my family."

"Do you expect to return to Morocco after a trip to America?"

"Yes, I will. The only family I have is here in this country."

The Chief of Police smiled, dismissed me and told me he would call me again if needed.

The ruler of the district also called me to his office. He questioned me, and I informed him that I taught the Word of God. "That is the work of the mosque teachers," he declared. I explained that those who came to my house were loyal to the king, the country and to God, and that they had high moral standards.

Before I left his office, he asked me what time we met and promised to drop in on the classes. I emphasized the women's and girls' classes, because I knew he would not enter a room where women were meeting. For security reasons, we held the fellowship meetings at night for a month, but he never visited.

Fearful after police had questioned people and searched homes in the early part of the summer of 1984, we tried to frustrate their attempts to find others of our group. We canceled meetings and classes at Derb Skat, often holding secret rendezvous, apprehensive about the future. In spite of the political situation, our house buzzed with activities during July. We had one week of day clubs for children, a week-long retreat for teenage girls, one week of camping with older teenage boys and a three- or four-day club for teenage boys. These were all taught by Moroccans, some of whom had reason to fear, such as Rachida, whom the authorities had sought but had not found, and Sidi Mustapha, whom they had sought and found before.

At the end of the summer, I had to say goodbye again and return to the United States. I had hesitated to take another furlough, afraid I might not get back into Morocco. But I needed to renew my relationship with my prayer partners. I had been away from the American culture again for too long, and since retirement was inevitable, I needed all the help I could get to learn to relate to the American public. My thinking, my dress, my interests, my speech and my habits were all affected by the culture I had adopted. I worried that I would not fit in.

There was the concern, too, about the doctor's report. To my relief and delight, he found no problem. I spent Christmas in Minnesota and bought my ticket to return to Morocco on March 4, 1985, two days before my sixty-eighth birthday. As the plane flew over the Atlantic, I had lots of time to think. My thoughts went not only to my family of believers but also to the millions in Morocco who didn't know about the saving power of our Lord Jesus. How could one think of settling down to a retired life of ease when so much needed to be done and there were so few to do the work?

Clearly, we needed to recruit new workers – creative missionaries who could find ways of entering Morocco other than with a missionary visa. Often the government would grant entry visas to those with special skills who were willing to take jobs as they became available. We had now grown to five team members in Morocco, three of us in Meknes. Together we set our goal to have fifteen new workers by 1990.

God had answered many, many prayers in my years of ministry in Morocco. I enthusiastically endorsed this goal, and I was ready to settle back into my limited but busy routine in Meknes, with my heart praising the Lord.

Leaving the Church in God's Hands

The believers had held Sunday services regularly in my absence with good attendance. The younger men were now learning to prepare devotional messages. I could see the results of good discipling by my co-worker. Sunday mornings at 10:00, a herd of students crowded in the door to attend three simultaneous classes. Some older fellows took over a class of promising teenage boys I had been trying to hold together for a few years. A young lady, a recent convert, taught three small children, and a young woman took over the teenage girls' class. Tuesday afternoons, we met in the home of a believer to study the book of Revelation.

So many individuals were asking for special studies that I wondered how I could handle them all on their level, but the Lord provided a way. A Southern Baptist missionary in Fes who had served in the Mideast had a good knowledge of the language and a pastor's heart. He made himself available to come to Meknes once a week for a two-hour Bible study. We arranged it so the students came every other week. One week he held a class in Old Testament studies for about eight students, the next week a class in the New Testament for about six. The latter group consisted of those who had not yet made a profession of faith but wanted to study.

The summer of 1989 was very special. God laid on my heart the burden to hold small retreats during the summer for children or younger siblings of believers to give them some good Bible teaching. All year they learned the Qur'an. One week was all we could afford or had time for. In the days of Sunset Farm we would simply have had to load them on a bus and transport them to Khemisset – to the huge, well-equipped farm, swimming pool, picnic yard, ball fields and swings. Because of the restrictions of the government, however, we could not conduct large groups without inspection. We had to limit the number to about ten at a time and call it a vacation. This limited the number to fifty children, whom we could fit into four weeks. Calls came in from believers in Fes, Casablanca, Rabat, Oujda and Ouarzazate. To whom could these believers go for spiritual guidance for their young ones but to us? We could not and we did not let them down.

Late that summer, the Fellowship group held a beautiful farewell for me. I had taken many mini-furloughs, but this was the big one. I was going home; no, I was leaving home, returning to America for good. Reluctantly I boarded the plane on August 26, 1989, after forty-three wonderful years in Morocco. I came back to the United States to begin a new life and a new ministry, but I left my heart behind.

Glossary of Foreign Words

ashkoon "Who?" "Who is at the door?"

cadi Muslim magistrate, judge.

caläche Small horse-drawn carriage.

caliph Ruler, deputy, vice-gerent, successor to the Prophet Muhammad.

couscous The national dish of Morocco, generally made from semolina (a coarse cream of wheat), but sometimes made from barley or cornmeal. When steamed, it resembles cooked rice in texture. It is steamed in a special container over a boiled dinner of meat or milk and vegetables. The meal is served in one large, flat dish, from which the entire family and guests partake.

dabeeha Sacrifice.

derb Dark, narrow alley that leads to the entrance of a house.

fez Red, round, tasseled woolen hat worn by Arab men living in the city.

hajj The fifth pillar of Islam, it is the pilgrimage to Mecca.

halfa Oath.

harera Vegetable soup with coriander base thickened with sourdough yeast.

henna The dried leaves of the henna plant, commonly used by Moroccan women as a hair dye and for medicinal purposes. On joyous occasions the feet and hands are decorated with artistic henna designs.

jelaba Floor-length cloak with a large hood. This garment is worn as a coat by both men and city women. The women, in addition, wear veils over the lower part of their faces.

kasbah Fortified city, fortress; old and crowded part of a North African city.

medina Ancient, walled-in Muslim section of a city.

mellah Jewish quarter of a city.

mizrug-allah Custom that obligates a host to protect his guests.

muezzin Person who calls the devout to prayer from the minaret of the mosque.

Nsara Christian (comes from "Nazarene").

nuala Round mud hut with a grass thatch roof.

Qur'an Koran, the holy book of the Muslim people.

salat The second pillar of Islam, it is prayer, practiced regularly by the very devout.

sawm The fourth pillar of Islam, it is Ramadan, or the fast.

serwelle An undergarment much like a mid-calf skirt sewn shut across the hemline with holes for the legs, worn by both men and women.

shahadah The first pillar of Islam, it is the creed or the witness to Allah and his Apostle Muhammad. It is the only absolute requirement to become a Muslim.

sugar cone Fine–quality sugar pressed into a large four–pound cone used by Moroccan families, rich and poor. A sugar cone is the proper gift to bring to one's host or hostess.

svenge Raised, unsweetened doughnut made early in the morning in open shops or marketplaces. *Svenge* is eaten primarily for breakfast but is sold all day long in the country markets.

ta-jeen Succulent food or stew; covered earthenware dish that holds this food.

zakat The third pillar of Islam, it is the giving of alms.

zamata Mealy mixture made of wheat flour, sugar, spices and oil or butter. This mixture is always made on the occasion of a birth and is said to have strengthening value for the new mother.